The Tragedy of the Revolution

The Tragedy of the Revolution

Adrian E. Cristobal

The University of the Philippines Press
Diliman, Quezon City

THE UNIVERSITY OF THE PHILIPPINES PRESS
E. de los Santos St., UP Campus, Diliman, Quezon City 1101
Tel. No.: 9253243 / Telefax No.: 9282558
e-mail: press@up.edu.ph / uppress@uppress.org
website: www.uppress.org

Book Design by Veni L. Ilowa

ISBN 971-542-471-6

Printed in the Philippines by NJP Printmakers Incorporated

Contents

In Search of the Hero

There is no life that can be recaptured wholly; as it was. Which is to say that all biography is fiction. What does that tell you about the nature of life, and does one really want to know?

Bernard Malamud, *Dubin's Lives*

We are always coming up with emphatic facts of history in our experience and verifying them here. All history becomes subjective—in other words, there is properly no history; only biography.

Ralph Waldo Emerson, *Essays on History*

Biographies are but the clothes and buttons of the man; the biography of the man himself cannot be written.

Mark Twain, *Autobiography*

Anyone of any consequence today deserves a biography. If he (or she) doesn't think so, his relatives and friends do. But there has grown a large market for biographies. People love to read about famous people, whatever the basis of fame. After all, celebrity is an achievement in itself.

It is ironic therefore, that among our national heroes, Andres Bonifacio is destitute of a *Life* in more than one sense: no memoirs, no diaries—his life was cut short. Scholars like Manuel Cuerva Artigas, Epifanio de los Santos y Cristobal and historian Teodoro Agoncillo wrote about him, basing their accounts on interviews, his letters, a few poems, a Decalogue, and a manifesto, reading into the scarce output a universe of meanings. This probably accounts for the familiar phenomenon of a brief poem yielding tomes of exegetical analysis. O. D. Corpuz devoted a paragraph on this life, although he located the hero in the sweeping saga of our people's pilgrimage to nationhood. The reason, of course, is that there is not much on Andres Bonifacio the man. The sparseness of biographical data is symbolic of his poverty.

As a result, scholars and historians adopted the strategy, in giving Bonifacio a life, of situating it in the history of the *Katipunan* and the Revolution. That Bonifacio was undoubtedly the father of the Katipunan and arguably of the Revolution as well (I argue here that he *is* the Revolution) does not make the biographical task easier.

On the contrary, it makes it impossible.

What, then, can be the reason for this book? I doubt its use for the scholar and the historian: I am neither. I say this not as an apology but as a warning. But I don't intend to unsettle the small legion of historians and historicists who have willy-nilly defined the *Great Plebeian* according to their lights. It is not that I disagree with their facts; I disagree with the significance, if any, that they have given to or extracted from the rudiments (or shall I say "remains") of Bonifacio's brief life.

There is another, perhaps more "elevated purpose" which shall be revealed in time.

Meanwhile, the title of this introduction is an invitation to those who, in some vague way, feel strongly about Andres Bonifacio. It also tries to explain an empathy rooted in childhood. Perhaps, being a denizen, at various stages in my life, of Tondo, Paco, Sta. Cruz (Bonifacio lived in Zurbaran while I lived in Mayhaligue, though obviously not at the same moment in time), and Sta. Ana accounts for my choice of hero. (Rizal is much admired but regrettably inaccessible, an Olympian among heroes, no matter how many times we tell ourselves that he is worthy of emulation. The *macabre* joke is that a combination of his genius and patriotism can lead but to the grave, even in these times.)

In my childhood, the games we played in the streets of Manila frequently echoed with the war cry *Sugod, mga kapatid!* (Advance, brothers!) To our childish minds not yet instructed in history, this was Bonifacio's

Cry of Balintawak, the Cry of the Revolution that resounds throughout our history. We learned later on in public school that the actual cry was *Mabuhay ang mga Anak ng Bayan!* (Long live the Sons of the People!) at one point, and *Mabuhay ang Filipinas!* at another; but this did not affect our attachment to *Sugod*. At this time too, we were intoning, for reasons that I cannot now recall, the revolutionary triad of our history: Rizal was the inspiration; Mabini, the brain; and Bonifacio, the arm of the Revolution.

I was later dissatisfied with this division and insisted that Bonifacio was the *heart* of the Revolution. Now, he *is* the Revolution.

At the same time, my public school generation took it for granted that Emilio Aguinaldo killed Andres Bonifacio, and not even our devil's advocate disagreed. By then not one of us regarded Aguinaldo as a hero, until further instruction persuaded us that he was, having stood up to the Americans, except that unlike Mabini, he did not take his time pledging allegiance to the United States.

Then I came across Teodoro Agoncillo's *The Revolt of the Masses*, which I thought an odd title for a conservative (others say "reactionary") classic denunciatory essay on the revolt of the masses. In any case, the Agoncillo book inspired me to write a play on the trial of Andres Bonifacio. Writing the play gave me some insights on the Revolution, which, in turn, goaded me to read as much as I could on the literature of revolutions.

I was content with this. Andres Bonifacio is history, all is right with the world. For a whole decade, I thought no more about it until I was shaken out of stupor by the controversies that began to emerge around the person of the Great Plebeian. I guess historians must always do history. They need to expose one another's weaknesses in the process of establishing their credentials. There is nothing reprehensible in this insofar as it is honest work. In any case, many of our historians are absolved: I reserve my spit for a particular American scholar who tried to tell us that Bonifacio was an "invented hero."

There was also partisanship that I never thought existed between the *Rizalistas* and the *Bonifacionados*, although I found many admirers of Rizal who were as equally admiring of Bonifacio. (The Aguinaldo advocates, I am sorry to say, are still struggling for respectability; although I am happy to say, they have officially prevailed with the transfer of Independence Day from July 4 to June 12, a high recognition for Aguinaldo's role in the making of the Filipino nation.)

Still on my very first lecture on Bonifacio, written in Tagalog and delivered at Liwasang Bonifacio under the auspices of the National Historical Institute, I was collared by a Bonifacio descendant who told me bluntly that Rizal was a "coward." I also stumbled into a Rizalist who thought that the Revolution was better off without Bonifacio! I realized then how much of our past is not yet history.

As generals continue to fight their last war, chroniclers and historians are reviewing Andres Bonifacio's "war record." If this is just to get at the truth of what really happened, it is of some service to researchers and students of history. But if from these bare facts, the idea is to show that Bonifacio deserved his fate in Cavite, then it does more harm than good in assaying the significance of the Revolution that he initiated.

Fortunately, another breed of historians stresses the superior odds that the Manila *Katipuneros* were up against, as the Spanish authorities had to defend Manila before the reinforcements from Spain would enable them to recapture the municipalities of Cavite. I do not mean to argue that Bonifacio was a Bolivar, but to fault him with tactical weakness is putting tactics in a situation to which it does not belong. Confined to a guerilla war, Bonifacio and the thousand or so "troops" directly under his eyes could only manage as best as they could. If he and his men had had the foresight to be well prepared, it is more than likely that our centennial as a nation would have to begin in 1945, the Liberation of Manila.

However (and this I stress), because of the uprising in Manila, the Revolution spread through the provinces, spurred by the news that the Revolution had struck at the center of power. This is not a total misimpression, since the Revolution erupted in Manila.

The comparison between failure "here" and success "there" is misleading in that it ignores the impetus of the Revolution. The Cry of Balintawak inspired those within hearing and knowing distance, so that even as Bonifacio and his men were besieged in the heart of the colonial power, thousands flocked to the Katipunan provincial and municipal councils, offering their lives to the Revolution. Distant chroniclers would argue that word about successes in the field of battle, of which Bonifacio had few, was crucial to the upsurge of revolutionary fervor. Not so. There was no media then, controlled or free. Rumors flew, contradicting each other, but people believed what they wanted to believe; and they believed that the train of Revolution was on the way and that they should be on it. The only word is that "the *Supremo* has done it, so let us do it!"

Now, is this fact or fantasy? Where are the documents, the letters, the interviews with the survivors? As if documents were the only proof of how people thought at a critical time. The eighteenth century classical scholar Richard Bentley (if we need experts) put the matter in this way: *"Reason and the facts outweigh a hundred manuscripts—no amount of learning or mastery of method will compensate for lack of common sense."*

To this essay then, I bring in a personal passion in examining an unexplained life, with, I hope, not a small amount of common sense. A definitive biography about our national hero is not possible now. Perhaps, further diggings into kept records will unearth more materials. For deeper research on the life of the neglected hero, our researchers should be given the ample material support that they have not received so far. Bonifacio's detractors have had a better deal.

This official neglect, one notes, had inflamed personal passions and generated bitter controversies. A major reason is that the descendants and partisans of what is aptly called the "Bonifacio Era" are understandably concerned with protecting revered reputations, something that can only be achieved at the expense of the reputations of others. Aguinaldos, Alejandrinos, Tironas, Noriels, Paternos, del Pilars, are just some of the names that surrounded the revolutionary life of the Great Plebeian. They all have their living branches. Some, like historians and chroniclers, are more sensitive than others.

I was gingerly asked by my publishers to avoid giving offense to others, since this book is designed for understanding. The problem is Andres Bonifacio was not, in the end, a conciliatory fellow, although the Katipunan would not have grown as it did under his leadership if he had been nothing more than an irascible, temperamental, and impulsive man that some people made him out to be. However, since controversy still rages, all I could promise is not to make it worse.

I leave it to the wise reader to decide whether I have succeeded in this effort.

Finally, the way we remember, regard, and understand the most "invisible," "silent," and controversial figure in our history, must say something about what we are and what, if at all, we want to be as a people. In the midst of contentions, my prayer is to contribute towards a better and hopefully, less contentious understanding.

I may make the effort, essay it, not as a historian or scholar—I am neither—but as a writer who early in life was fascinated by this Man of the People—**Andres Bonifacio**, *El Supremo*, the Man who made Revolution.

A.E.C.

The Tragedy of the Revolution

CHAPTER ONE

Birth of a Hero

A ndres Bonifacio was born on 7 July 1892. He was then 28 years old—two years older than Apolinario de la Cruz, a year younger than Father Jose Burgos, and seven years younger than Dr. Jose Rizal when they were killed by the Spaniards: de la Cruz in 1841, Burgos in 1872, and Rizal in 1896.

Hermano Pule (as de la Cruz, the man from Lucban, Tayabas was called) organized the Cofradía de Señor San Jose, a religious fraternity that staged an uprising that claimed the life of a provincial governor. Father Jose Burgos, son of a Spanish colonel and a Spanish mestiza, was allegedly framed as the leader of the famous Cavite mutiny. Dr. Jose Rizal was marked as an enemy of Spain ever since he wrote about the abuses of colonial authorities, particularly the ecclesiastical.

Pule was drawn and quartered; Burgos was strangulated by garrote along with alleged co-conspirators, Fathers Mariano Gomez and Jacinto Zamora; and Rizal was shot in Bagumbayan.

Rebellion is the common denominator of Bonifacio and these three martyrs of the race, but Bonifacio is the exemplary revolutionary. Pule merely wanted to serve the God that the Spanish friars preached to the *indios*; Burgos championed the secularization of the clergy; Rizal crusaded for reforms. Any deviation from the prevailing orthodoxy was regarded by the authorities as a sedition.

Occurring more than half a century before the Katipunan Revolution, Hermano Pule's uprising, although disturbing to the Spaniards, was dismissed by them as a superstitious and fanatical phenomenon. In their view, the real danger came from the Filipino Spaniards (Spaniards born in the Philippines or who came to the colony at an early age) who were resentful of the *peninsulares* shipped out to the archipelago to occupy government positions. They were doubly dangerous when they were educated, (Rizal's hero in the novel *Noli Me Tangere*, the European-bred Crisostomo Ibarra, was the son of a Spaniard. More dangerous still if they were native and educated, as the *ilustrados* were. In this case, they were *filibusteros*, ironically but aptly defined by Rizal as "candidates for execution."

It is an old rule among colonial rulers to be suspicious of anyone with the ability to think for themselves. As the wise Sinibaldo de Mas (in Blair and Robertson), a Spanish diplomat and adviser put it in 1841: "The farmer or the goatherd does not read social contracts" (a clear reference to Rousseau, author of *The Social Contract* and the ideological father of the French Revolution) and "they are ignorant of happenings outside their village." They are not "the class of people who overthrew absolutism in Spain but the class educated in the colleges." These are the true enemies of Spain, people with liberal ideas. In the colonies, de Mas pronounced, a "liberal is synonymous with insurgent."

The "ignorant and lazy" indio must not be exposed to liberal ideas, otherwise he would recover his broken pride and fancy himself an equal of his Spanish master. Hermano Pule was exposed to this appalling idea, for he thought himself worthy enough to form a religious organization and Father Jose Burgos was among the harbingers. So was Rizal, who was first exposed to education and then infected his fellow indios. All three represented a type—disturber of the peace who must be eliminated.

There is an ideological connection between the deaths of Hermano Pule, Father Jose Burgos, Dr. Jose Rizal, and the birth of Bonifacio at age 28. The seventh of July 1892 was the precise date on which the Katipunan, the Highest and Most Honorable Association of the Sons of the People (*Kataastaasan Kagalang-galangang Katipunan ng Mga Anak ng Bayan*) was born.

Before his birth in the Katipunan, Andres Bonifacio's biological birth on 30 November 1863 merely made him one of the millions of indios whose "pride should be broken."

No distinction applied to his father, Santiago Bonifacio, and his mother, Catalina de Castro. But their early deaths abruptly ended Andres' schooling—(no higher than grade four, according to Agoncillo, but a little beyond, in Epifanio de los Santos judgment. Andres had to work in order to support his siblings: three brothers Procopio, Ciriaco, and Troadio, and two sisters Maxima and Esperidiona, who became the wife of one of the organizers of the Katipunan, Teodoro Plata.

Andres sold canes and paper fans, acted in zarzuelas, and did messengerial and trading work for an English firm called Fleming & Co. From this, historians and biographers deduced that he could at least speak some English, perhaps as well as many Filipinos today speak the language. There is no doubt, however, that he could read Spanish, for all the books discovered in his small library at the Fressel warehouse, were either written or translated into Spanish. He also wrote the best *first* Tagalog translation of *Mi Ultimo Adios*.

He "went without sleep at night in order to read" and loved to talk about the French Revolution. This "almost semi-literate warehouseman" actually got to third year high school in one of Manila's private schools, according to *Katipunero* Dr. Pio Valenzuela. This discrepancy is of no consequence since Mabini himself did not consider Andres Bonifacio "less instructed" than those who looked down on his lack of learning.

Bonifacio founded the Katipunan on the day of Rizal's deportation to Dapitan. The *La Liga Filipina*, formed by Rizal upon his return from Spain, almost died at birth. Apparently, the Katipunan was formed to replace La Liga since it was already exposed to the authorities. A secret society was needed to carry on the mission to "unite the archipelago into one compact, vigorous, and homogenous body."

This mission sounded seditious, so reformists like Deodato Arellano, the first president of the Katipunan, believed that the KKK should simply raise funds to support the propaganda organ, *La Solidaridad*, published in Spain by the *Indios Bravos*, the ilustrados whose names are bywords in Philippine history: Marcelo H. del Pilar, Graciano Lopez-Jaena, and Rizal himself.

The Katipunan members, all working class, balked at the idea, concluding, as Rizal and del Pilar did, that the Spaniards could no longer be won by words.

For this reason, the attempt to revive the Liga failed, although Bonifacio served as its propagandist and organizer at the same time that he was recruiting members for the Katipunan. The urban masses that he had recruited obviously wanted a revolutionary society, exactly reflecting his own sentiments.

Bonifacio recruited from people he knew best, having lived with them for years: urban workers in printing shops, courts, government offices, in the military and police (the *Guardia Civil*)—"not a single rich man nor one of a learned profession." Attests Isabelo de los Reyes: "I have said, and I will repeat a thousand times that the Katipunan was a plebeian society." He needn't be so vehement, for although Bonifacio was a member of La Liga Filipina, he was not himself an ilustrado but a working man, a *bodeguero* in a brick factory. His associations could not have been anything else but plebeian, *masa*. It must be noted, however, that the Supreme Council had one "learned man"—Dr. Pio Valenzuela.

Apolinario Mabini noted in his memoirs that the reformists "recognized for the first time that as regards to political aspirations, the popular masses, whom the Spaniards considered as insensible or at least indifferent, occupied the front ranks."

Nearly three years later in April 1895, Bonifacio, who had adopted the striking nom de guerre *Maypagasa* (With Hope) led a band of Katipuneros to the Montalban hills to initiate new members. In the Pamitinan cave, the Katipuneros scratched in coal the first cry of liberty and independence —*¡Viva la Independencia de Filipinas!* This bold move in the Pamitinan cave captured the imagination of the masses.

There followed a harvest of new members from Nueva Ecija, Bulacan, and Cavite, among them Emilio Aguinaldo y Famy, who was initiated in the Mason-like initiation rites, adopting the nom de guerre *Magdalo*, after the patron saint of Cavite del Viejo (Kawit), Mary Magdalene. By the time elections were held in Bonifacio's house on Zurbaran street in Santa Cruz on New Year's Day in 1896, the Association was able to count on the attendance of 200 of 300 initiated members. Andres Bonifacio was elected Supremo, and the brilliant (he was even regarded a genius) nineteen-year-old, pre-law student at the University of Santo Tomas, Emilio Jacinto Pedernal, as second man or *lottery prize*

Fiscal in the Supreme Council. A "secret chamber" was also formed with Bonifacio, Jacinto, and Dr. Pio Valenzuela.

This was the turning point in the dramatic saga of the Katipunan. It acquired a printing press through the generosity of two patriots from Kalibo, Capiz (now Aklan), Francisco del Castillo and Candido Iban, who donated 400 of the 1,000 pesos they had between them. They earned the money as sea-divers in Australia, although another account claims that they won it from a lottery. Whatever the provenance of the money, the Aklanons' nobility did not end there. They gave their lives as well to the revolutionary struggle in Kalibo.

Possessed of a printing press, the Katipunan could now have an organizing paper, the indispensable tool of all revolutionary movements. It was named *Kalayaan* (Freedom, Liberty). But first they had to scrounge for typefaces. Jacinto went to his mother, Josefa Dizon, for twenty pesos to buy all the available types in Isabelo de los Reyes' printing press. For four pesos a day, four employees of the *Diario de Manila* press brought in more types to Dr. Pio Valenzuela. However, Aguedo del Rosario and Apolonio de la Cruz gave additional types from the same *Diario* at no cost at all. Whether they bought the types themselves or "commandeered" them in the name of the Katipunan is a matter of conjecture. More likely, the *Diario* management was as negligent as the Filipino workers were resourceful.

Only one issue of *Kalayaan* was distributed: 200 copies for Cavite, 100 for Bulacan, and 700 for Manila. All copies were paid for by the recipients, but there was no accounting for the remaining 1,000 copies. Marcelo H. del Pilar, tubercular in Barcelona, was listed as editor in order to mislead the authorities, but the real editor was Emilio Jacinto, who traveled, after classes, from Magdalena street in Santa Cruz to Lavezares street in Tondo. The del Pilar ruse worked, for many Bulakeños who were conversant with Plaridel's Tagalog prose swore that Jacinto's language resembled the former's "perfectly."

A second issue was undistributed because of the discovery of the Association of the Sons of the People. Still, it was noted that from mid-March, when the first and only issue was distributed, to August 1896 (a five-month period) the Katipunan membership swelled to 30,000. Tarlac, Cavite, Bulacan, Nueva Ecija, Pampanga, Batangas, Laguna, and Manila (then a province) accounted for the membership; hence their recognition as the eight original provinces of the Revolution.

Along with the publication of *Kalayaan*, a change in the structure of the Katipunan from the Masonic "triad"—three members recruiting three members each, these three recruiting another three, etc. without the layers knowing one another—to Manila's supreme, provincial, and municipal councils, facilitated the growth in membership.

By the time of the traditional May festival of the Virgin of Antipolo, Bonifacio was able to summon the heads of sixty councils to the house of Valentin Cruz behind the Pasig church. He then announced to the assembly that the Katipunan was like a pregnant woman faced with a premature delivery. The reason for this was the vigilance of Governor General Ramon Blanco's spies. The Sons of the People now had to confront the revolutionary moment.

There are as many theories of revolution as there are opinion-makers, but all agree that there is an incubation period brought about by an atmosphere. "Revolution must be in the air." The question is how many would discern and follow it at the risk of "life, liberty, and sacred honor?" After watching the vicissitudes of the propagandists from afar and being shocked by Rizal's deportation to Dapitan, Bonifacio clearly saw the necessity of making revolution.

How Andres Bonifacio (often called El Supremo) was born to revolution was due to a combination of two factors: the circumstances of his life and experience, and his readings. Millions of people of his class undoubtedly suffered under Spanish rule, but only Bonifacio had the courage, the imagination, and the leadership qualities to take the first step of organizing a secret, revolutionary society.

It is difficult enough even in these days of peace to form an organization that can survive the diversity and eccentricities of individual members. It is nearly impossible to lead a secret society of deprived, desperate men and women, moved by anger and hate and yet goaded by fear, if not for country or themselves, for their loved ones. It would take a man of extraordinary talent to make suffering a common bond among such a diverse group of people whose singular thread lay only in their social origins.

Bonifacio had therefore ample opportunity to listen to his social and, let us say, intellectual "betters" discuss the suffering of his country and the ways that could be pursued in alleviating them. But some fraternal members did talk about revolution. Found in Bonifacio's "small archives" was the *kundiman* written by Rizal with the concluding lines:

O, happy is the man
Who would liberate her!

The evils of society have their origin in unbridled desires and lusts (the offsprings and companions of ignorance), which follies can be corrected only when the prudent and the circumspect are the rulers of the human throng instead of the imposters and the hypocrites. Unfortunately, the general run of humanity is usually ruled and led by men superior in craft and intellect (or malice) to the rest of the people whom they subjugate and exploit.

Ruins of Palmyra (also entitled *Meditations on the Revolution of the Empires*) was a book that was in vogue in Bonifacio's time. Describing the Revolution of 1789, this book postulated revolution as the supreme remedy to the ills of subjugation, exploitation, and repression, and became like fuel added to the flames.

Taken together with his other books, it is reasonable to believe that Bonifacio's readings gave him the idea of revolution. Epifanio de los Santos obviously saw great significance in the fact that Eugene Sue's *Wandering Jew* and the *Ruins of Palmyra** (whose author was not named)

---

*After publication of the first edition of *The Tragedy of the Revolution* I stumbled upon the information, while browsing the internet (which I confess I should have done earlier), that the book, its true title in English as *The Ruins, A Mediation on the Revolutions of Empires* (*Les Ruins, ou meditations sur les revolutions des empires*), was written by the French philosopher and historian, Constantin Francois Chasseboeuf Volney (1757-1820). According to Brian Rigby, the author of "Volney's Rationalist Apocalypse" presented at the *1789: Reading Writing Revolution, Proceedings of the Essex Conference on the Sociology of Literature* in July 1981, "Volney advocates that the people unite in order to cast off the remnants of a once mighty, but now fractured and decayed civilization, in order to establish a new worldwide order of reason and equality." *The Ruins* was published in 1791 and was translated anonymously in England the next year. Thomas Jefferson translated the first twenty chapters for an American edition. Highly influential in both nations, new editions and translations were published throughout the nineteenth and twentieth century.

were Bonifacio's favorites. In his book, *The Revolutionists*, de los Santos took special pains to ask: "Did not all this, coupled with the doctrines of *El Filibusterismo*, which novel Andres Bonifacio preferred to the *Noli*, presage the advent of the *Katipunan*?"

Presage indeed, but it would be different to say that books prepared Andres Bonifacio for revolution rather than that he had been prepared for these books. It was not for learning and instruction but for inspiration that the Father of the Revolution read them.

By the time Andres Bonifacio had grown to manhood, he had his fill of what is now called "protest literature." This literature gave a coherent shape and confirmation to his experience as an ordinary workingman from Tondo. For all of Rizal's cautionary words in *El Filibusterismo*, which Bonifacio cherished above the more polished and engaging *Noli Me Tangere*, none but a reader for entertainment's sake could miss the undercurrent, running through its pages, of the moral and logical necessity of revolution. In a word, the Spanish rulers, through political and ecclesiastical power, turned the vanquished into criminals and heretics then punished them for being such.

Rizal "killed" the vindictive Simoun (Ibarra in disguise) because his "revolution" was based on aggravating the sufferings of his countrymen. As Simoun told the young medical student Basilio:

> *Summoned by the vices of those who rule, I have returned and, beneath a businessman's cloak, I have traversed the towns. With my wealth I have opened the way, and wherever I have been, greed in the most execrable forms, now hypocritical, now shameless, now cruel, feeds on a dead organism like a vulture devouring a cadaver. And I have asked myself, why the poison, the toxins, the venom of the graves, do not ferment in its guts, to kill the loathsome bird? The corpse is left destroyed; the vulture is satiated with flesh, and since it is not possible for me to give it life so that it would turn against its executioner, and since corruption sets in gradually, I have incited greed; I have favored it; the injustices and abuses I have multiplied; I have fomented crime, the acts of cruelty to accustom the people to the prospect of death; I have encouraged anxiety so that flight from it would lead to any solution whatsoever. I have placed*

obstacles to commerce so that the country, made poor and reduced to misery, would fear nothing. I have instigated ambitions to impoverish the treasury; and this being sufficient to lead to a popular uprising, I have wounded the people in their most sensitive fibers; I have driven the vulture itself to degrade the same cadaver that gives it life and corrupts it ...

Here, Rizal bitterly insinuates that the people have not suffered enough to strike at the vulture. At the same time, his solution was to educate them for freedom, obviously contradicting Simoun's vision of a merely enraged populace. But as Bonifacio saw it, the people, like him, were enraged enough. They knew no French but their cry echoed that of the *sans culottes*—*Ecrasez l'infame!* Death to infamy!

Life and literature formed the womb of revolutionary thought. Indeed, revolution is first a thought, a word that arises, above all, from feeling.

Here we go back to Sinibaldo de Mas, our adviser of 1841, who advocated in a secret memo the "emancipation" of the Philippines by Spain. Observing that the repressive measures and administrative reforms he proposed for the "conservation of the colony" could not be implemented, fearing that the Philippines "will emancipate itself violently with the loss of considerable property and many lives of European Spaniards and Filipinos," he proposed that:

It would be infinitely more easy for us to acquire the glory of the world by being the first to show generosity. Hence, the foreign authors who have unjustly printed so many calumnies against our colonial governments, authors belonging to nations who never satisfy their hunger for colonies, would have to say at least this once:

The Spaniards, crossing new and remote seas, extended the domain of geography by discovering the Filipinas islands. They found anarchy and despotism there, and established order and justice. They encountered slavery and destroyed it, and imposed political equality. They ruled their inhabitants with laws, and just laws. They Christianized them, civilized them, defended them from the Chinese, from Moro pirates and from European aggressions; they spent much gold on them, and then gave them liberty.

These were precisely the demands of the propagandist-ilustrados, to which Mother Spain did not listen as she did not listen to Sinibaldo de Mas. How astutely Mabini put it in his *Revolucion Filipina*:

> *The* Katipunan *spread very rapidly, because the insolent and provoking manner in which the friars conducted their campaign of opposition had exasperated the popular masses; but if the organization of political societies had then been permitted in the Archipelago and the middle class, which was the most educated and influential, had been able to move freely, there is no doubt that the popular resentment could have been calmed and the growth of the Katipunan prevented, because that class was resolutely in favor of the program of the Liga, even after they had passed through most cruel torments, and still more after the Biac-na-Bato treaty.*

Undoubtedly, Andres Bonifacio and the people respected and trusted the middle class to lead them to the Promised Land of freedom and justice, but they saw that the class was being decimated for advocating reforms. In the process, their mass followers were also being tortured, butchered, and deported. It dawned on the Great Plebeian that since reforms were branded revolutionary, then revolution was the only avenue for their attainment.

The Program of the Katipunan, or the *Kartilya*, under Article IV encouraged members to go abroad in order to procure arms and "other necessary articles," and after acquiring them, "convene and discuss feasible means to gain the redemption of our enslaved Motherland through the muzzles of rifles and cannons."

Recruits were initiated in elaborate ceremonies. Blindfolded, they entered the house of initiation where they were presented before the "directors of the Association." The Program of the Katipunan was placed on a human skull on a table before them. Putting their hands on the skull, they recited the oath:

> *In the name of the Motherland, I join the Katipunan and I swear with all my heart that I will comply with all my duties and obligations as a true*

son who will defend her rights and never betray her until she is freed from the bondage of foreigners.

Significantly, the word "foreigners" was used instead of "Spaniards." Section 1 of Article I stipulated that all members should be native-born in the country.

They signed the oath in blood and were forbidden to reveal their true names to anyone; hence, the use of nomes de guerre.

After taking the oath, members were read the Program and assigned their duties without, however, knowing the person to whom they had sworn.

Then the admonition:

We, the sons of the Motherland, have established this society for her sake and in order to redeem her; and because of this, it is very necessary that we be united in a fraternal association to help one another in any emergency; to bear in mind always that we are of the same color and race. This is our true origin: we are related to each other, not only as relatives but also as true brothers, sons of a common mother.

To recognize one another, Katipuneros were instructed on the secret hand signs: members of the first degree clenched their right hand with the thumb extended; of the second degree, clenched hand with the thumb on top of the index finger; and of the third degree, clenched hand with the thumb, index and middle fingers extended.

All members must strive to eliminate disunity among themselves so that we can accomplish our desired end.

A striking provision was the interdict on wives and daughters of Katipuneros from going to confession, lest the Association be compromised.

If moral resolution (which means a pledged mind and heart) is part of revolutionary preparedness, certainly the Katipuneros were prepared.

Born into history on 7 July 1892, Andres Bonifacio, the hero, rose to manhood on the August week, 23 to 29, 1896, initiating the most glorious period of Philippine history and the Revolution. Indeed, Andres Bonifacio is the Katipunan is the Revolution.

CHAPTER TWO

The Making of the Revolutionist

W hy does a person become a revolutionist? When a revolution comes, it attracts hundreds and thousands, probably all with different motives but united under one common cause. But the man who makes revolution must be moved by something deeper than a desire to do "something historic." Scholars of revolutions inevitably turn to the biographies of revolutionary leaders, hoping to find in them the one extraordinary element that makes them different from ordinary men.

There is often discovered a personal experience of injustice. It is a truism that the comfortable, the untouched, are not possessed by the passion to overthrow the existing order. They have no reason to.

Twentieth-century revolutionists like Vladimir Lenin and Mao Ze Dong had personal grievances against the existing order. Lenin saw his brother, Peter, publicly hanged by orders of the Tzar. Mao had seen too many injustices committed against his friends, neighbors, and countrymen. All the same, many others have suffered greater injustices and sufferings without turning to revolution.

Rizal, as well as his companions in the Propaganda, did not lack personal reasons for overturning the colonial order: not only did he suffer insult and injury as a young student in Manila but his family, particularly his mother, suffered physically and economically in the hands of the friar corporations and the alferez. Still, in spite of the fact that his writings showed the inherent corruption and injustice of colonialism, his response was to work for reforms. As an enlightened man, he was against the use of violence to achieve political aims. He was not, however, a pacifist, for he was not above challenging the Spanish historian, Wenceslao Retana, to a duel for making insulting remarks about his family. But like many of his countrymen, he understood the terrible consequences of revolution on the innocent. Fathers Gomez, Burgos, and Zamora, and many prominent citizens, were not involved in the Cavite mutiny of 1872; still, the government insisted on their guilt and sentenced them to death by strangulation at the garrote. It was the policy to keep the indios in a permanent state of terror by the persecution of those whom they respected or admired.

Revolts were a motif of Spanish rule in the Philippines, but they were no more than disturbances in the eyes of the authorities, although they were alert to the slightest restlessness "among the natives." (The exception was the intransigence of the Muslims—whose greatest leader was the legendary Sultan Kudarat—and the Igorots and Negritos, a reflection of their distrust of "Christian civilization"). This was the reason for the policy of continuing repression in the form of arrests and deportations. While the "ignorant and indolent indios" were incapable of thoughts of emancipation, they could be moved by the chimeras of the "disillusioned" educated class.

There was always something to revolt against: taxation, forced labor, or the tyranny and avarice of the friars. The heirs of Lakandula and Soliman revolted because the Spaniards did not exempt them from forced labor, tributes, and other taxes. Bohol's Francisco Dagohoy (1744) revolted because the friars refused his brother a Christian burial; his rebellion lasted for eighty-five years, outlasting the shorter life of its leader. On the other hand, fellow Boholano Tamblot (1621) and Bangkaw of Limasawa (1622) wanted to restore pre-Spanish worship.

Francisco Maniego of Pampanga (1660) and Andres Malong of Pangasinan, Ilokos, rose against forced labor. Malong's resistance spread to Pampanga, Zambales, and Cagayan. In 1762, it was the famed Juan de la Cruz Palaris, again against tributes and corruption.

Finally, there was the Diego Silang revolt which spread to Pangasinan and the Cagayan Valley; he succeeded for a while in establishing the local government of Vigan. However, exhorted by Bishop Ustarriz, the Ilocanos turned against Silang, and he was assassinated by his old friend,

Pedro Becbec, with the assistance of a mestizo named Miguel Vicos. His widow Gabriela Silang resumed the revolt but was defeated by the government with the help of native soldiers. No revolt seems to escape treachery in one form or another at the hands of fellow countrymen.

Even by word of mouth, the repercussions of these revolts shaped the consciousness of informed Filipinos. The enlightened class clearly understood the sentiments of those who participated in the revolts, but they would not do so far as to consider these as the "precursors" of the Revolution, as we do now. They were signs of discontent, to be sure, but the way to prevent them was for Spain to heed the cry of the oppressed and act according to her Catholic conscience. Moreover, there were also prominent Spaniards who were sympathetic to the Filipinos' cause, although the astute Sinibaldo de Mas observed that the volatility of Madrid politics argued against the successful implementation of reforms.

Above all, the fate of all revolts showed that they were more damaging to the natives than to their masters. Without the leadership of an enlightened class, no revolt had any chance of becoming a revolution. Peasants rise in revolt, but revolutions at any time were led and instigated by the lettered middle-class and even aristocrats. In the case of the French Revolution, historians pointed to the disillusionment of the intellectuals and the betrayal of the nobles of their class.

In Cuba, people of Spanish blood and lineage overthrew the colonial government. Like the American Revolution, it was an "insurrection in the family." People of color were just in the revolutionary periphery, at best.

Where, then, does one locate Andres Bonifacio's passion for revolution? He could have suffered personal insult, as suggested by his aborted plan to assassinate the parish *cura* of Tondo, Mariano Gil. The urban poor recruited were for revolution, but it can only be guessed at whether they came to the conclusion themselves or through the appeals of Bonifacio. The safest guess is that they were just waiting for the leader who could put their sentiments into words and unify them to collective action. Caught in the vortex of the Katipunan's discovery, they reached the end of their tether.

But there is nothing in Bonifacio's writings that alluded to a personal injury in the hands of the cura or the authorities. It is so different in the case of Jose Rizal, who left ample evidence of his sensitivity and melancholia about his own and his country's sufferings. However, research by E. Arsenio Manuel revealed that Hermogenes Bonifacio, elder brother of Bonifacio's father, Santiago, was arrested by the *Guardia Civil Veterana* in their house in Tondo. The unfortunate uncle had gone there ostensibly to help his younger brother in the making of fans and canes. It turned out that he had escaped from the dreaded *polos*, the forced labor in public works, and also the *quintos*, forced military service. He was banished to Puerto Princesa, Palawan, where his wife joined him when she found out much later where he was.

Revolution was "in the air," but only Bonifacio breathed it in. It happened that he was a Tondo boy, a denizen of the city, the heart of colonial power. The city is the place where revolutions begin, as they began in Paris, Shanghai, St. Petersburg, and in a recent pseudo-revolutionary case, EDSA. Only contemporary revolutionary theory speaks of surrounding the citadel of power from the countryside.

The accepted explanation is that, like Rizal and Marcelo H. del Pilar (accounts differ—each accused the other of pursuing fruitless reforms in Madrid rather than in the home country), Bonifacio arrived at the revolutionary junction out of the failure of the Propaganda and the ruins of La Liga Filipina. This explanation diminished both the revolutionary fervor of Bonifacio and the decisive role of the Propaganda in arousing the anger of the Filipinos against Spanish rule. For all the avowed peaceful intentions of the Indios Bravos, the Spanish authorities were not deceived into thinking that their writings were meant to foster brotherly love between Spaniards and Filipinos. The ilustrados in exile could have employed the elegant, non-confrontational language of Sinibaldo de Mas, who advocated the "emancipation of the Philippines," than the blistering satires of Rizal, del Pilar, and Lopez Jaena, if that was, indeed, their intention. That they did not call the oppressed to arms, and used the pen instead of the sword, could not have convinced the authorities that their words pacified their countrymen or sustained their dreams of peaceful reforms.

"What is a rebel?" asks the French Nobel Laureate Albert Camus in his classic essay, "The Rebel."

> *A man who says no, but whose refusal does not imply a renunciation. He is also a man who says yes, from the moment he makes his first gesture of rebellion. A slave who has taken orders all his life suddenly decides that he cannot obey some new command. What does he mean by saying "no?"*
>
> *He means, for example, that "this has been going on too long," "up to this point yes, beyond it, no," "you are going too far," or, again, "there is a limit beyond which you shall not go." In other words, his "no" affirms the existence of a borderline ... He demonstrates, with obstinacy, that there is something in him which is "worthwhile..." and which must be taken into consideration. In a certain way, he confronts an order of things which oppresses him with the insistence on a kind of right not to be oppressed beyond the limit that he can tolerate.*

To put it another way, revolution does not intrude into a man's mind by a cold intellectual process of observation to conclusion. It does not capture the minds and hearts of a group of men after a series of seminars and discussions. It comes not as orderly thought but, if you will, disorderly feeling. Revolution is a logic of chaos. The revolutionist, the revolutionary leader, must, however, give it form. Here the words are important, and Andres Bonifacio had them.

But the words were not the words of the Propaganda. He, of course, had imbibed them, but the superbly written articles were various and lengthy, and since he was not writing an academic paper, he needed something more concise, compelling, and readily grasped. The result was *Ang Dapat Mabatid ng mga Tagalog.* The English translation is "What the Tagalogs Should Know," but *batid* goes beyond knowledge: it is profound realization, an understanding that goes to the roots of one's soul. In acquiring this batid, one is not merely intellectually satisfied but existentially mobilized. One doesn't say, "I see," but "My God, yes!" It is akin to the discovery of love, except that it is love of country.

Conceivably, Bonifacio, in writing *Ang Dapat Mabatid* borrowed from Jose Rizal's annotation of the Spanish historian Morga's bland assertion that pre-Spanish Philippines was bereft of civilization. Rizal countered that the inhabitants of pre-Spanish Philippines had not only an alphabet but also customs and manners which marked an indigenous civilization.

As a revolutionist rather than a scholar, Bonifacio transformed Rizal's argument into a vision of an Eden-like community cruelly and cynically despoiled by the Spaniards. It is said that popular revolutions contain an element of nostalgia for an ideal past. The Spanish words *revolto* and *revolver* imply "return" as well as "revolve," while the Tagalog word *himagsik* involves an *up-rising* from an abject state in which one did not originally belong.

Decidedly, there is an echo here of Rousseau's striking observation that "Man was born free but everywhere he is chains."

It can be argued that the idea of Eden came from the proselytizing Spaniards, but every culture has a golden age, which is a constant reproach on the present. Out of this native sense of lost innocence, Bonifacio made the *Pacto de Sangre*, the blood compact between Legazpi and Sikatuna, the scorching metaphor of betrayal and redemption, treachery and revolution.

In five paragraphs of varying length, Bonifacio summed up the history of the race from the coming of the Spaniards to the urgent hour of redemption. He depicted a happy, prosperous community that welcomed the intruder who proclaimed that he came in peace and submitted himself to the old Tagalog's pledge of loyalty and mutual help through the blood compact. But the Spaniards, by deceit and force, took advantage of the natives' goodwill and enslaved them.

It is impossible to translate the emotional power of Bonifacio's short manifesto, in which he described the sacrifices of his countrymen to promote the Spanish "friend" in riches and comfort, for which they received as payment the tears of men, women, and children, separated by imprisonment, exile, and death. He does not ask for liberty, freedom of the press, representation in the Spanish *Cortes*, all democratic institutions, but for the righting of wrongs and the punishment of those whose pledge proved false. A betrayal of trust, of friendship so vital in the common life of the Tagalogs.

The Pacto de Sangre is also the undying pledge of the Katipunero, signified by a scar on the wrist that identified, and later exposed hundreds of Filipinos to Spanish soldiers and friars. In the very act of infliction, the initiate reminds himself of two things: the Spaniards' betrayal of a sacred oath and his own pledge to honor it to the end of his days. The pact, so betrayed by a foreigner, is now restored in its proper place: in the heart of the Katipunero.

In all revolutionary societies, treachery is the one unforgivable offense. Andres Bonifacio related the revolutionary code to the treachery of the Spaniards, and by the blood compact, injected it into the veins of the Katipunero. Without this ritual, enshrined in the memory of the race, admission into the revolutionary society would have been deprived of its solemnity. The upper or educated classes would have found this "bloodletting" a theatrical gesture irrelevant to commitment, but the humbler classes took ferocious pride in it.

Later on, the Pacto de Sangre was dispensed with to facilitate the admission of those who wanted to fight in late August 1896, when a *Katagalugan* revolutionary government was established in place of the Katipunan.

Back to *Ang Dapat Mabatid*, Teodoro A. Agoncillo and Silvino V. Epistola offered a translation that gives accurate information about its contents:

> *The Filipinos, who in early times were governed by our true countrymen before the coming of the Spaniards, were living in great abundance and prosperity. They were at peace with the inhabitants of the neighboring countries, especially with the Japanese with whom they traded and exchanged goods of all kinds. The means of livelihood increased tremendously, and for this reason, everybody had nobility of heart, whilst young and old, including the women, knew how to read and write in our autochthonous alphabet. The Spaniards came and offered us friendship. The self-governing people, because they were ably convinced that we shall be guided toward a better condition and led to a path of knowledge, were crumpled by the honeyed words of deceit. Even so, they (the Spaniards) were obliged to follow the customs of the Filipinos, their agreement having been sealed and made binding*

by means of an oath that consisted in taking a quantity of blood from each other's vein, and drinking it, as a token of their true and loyal promise not to be faithless to what had been agreed upon. This was called the Blood Compact of King Sikatuna and Legazpi, who represented the King of Spain.

More than three hundred years have elapsed since then, and for that length of time we have been bountifully supplying the needs of Legazpi's countrymen, we have been feeding them lavishly, even if we had to suffer privation and extreme hunger, we have spent our wealth, blood and life itself in their defense; we even went so far as to fight our own countrymen who refused to submit to them; and likewise, we combated the Chinese and the Dutch who attempted to wrest the Philippines from them.

Now, for all this, what is the tangible concession that has been bestowed upon our country in exchange for what we have done? What do we see in the way of keeping faith with their promise that was the cause of our sacrifices? None but treachery is the reward for our manifesto, and instead of keeping their promise that we would be led to the path of knowledge, they have blinded us and contaminated us with their meanness of character and forcibly destroyed the sanctity of our country's customs. We have been nurtured in a false belief and the honor of our people has been dragged into the mire of evil. And if we dare beg for a little love, they retaliate by banishing us and tearing us away from our beloved children, wives, and aged parents. Every sigh that escapes our breast is branded as a grave sin and is immediately punished with brute ferocity.

Now nothing can be considered stable in our lives; our peace is now always disturbed by the moans and lamentations, by the sighs and griefs of innumerable orphans, widows, and parents of the countrymen who were wronged by the Spanish usurpers; now we are being deluged by the streaming tears of a mother whose son was put to death, by the wails of tender children orphaned by cruelty and whose every tear that falls is like molten lead that scars the painful wound of our suffering hearts; now we are more and more being bound with the chains of slavery, chains that are shameful to every man of honor. What, then, must we do? The sun of reason that shines in the East clearly shows to our eyes that have been long blinded the path that we ought to follow: by its light we can see the claws of cruelty threatening us with death. Reason tells us that we cannot expect anything but more and more sufferings, more and more treachery, more and more insults, and more and more slavery. Reason teaches us to rely on ourselves and not to depend on others for our living. Reason tells us to be united in sentiment, in thought, and in purpose in order that we may have the strength to find the means of combating the prevailing evils of society.

It is now time for the light of truth to shine; it is now time for us to show that we have feelings, honor, shame, and mutual cooperation. Now is the time to commence the diffusion of the noble and great gospel that will rend asunder the thick curtain that obfuscates our minds; now is the time for Filipinos to know the sources of their misfortunes. Now is the time to realize that for every move we make we are stepping on and heading toward the brink of the abyss of death that our enemies have dug to ensnare us.

Therefore, O my countrymen! Let us open the eyes of our minds and voluntarily consecrate our strength to what is good in the true and full faith that the prosperity of the land of our birth, which is aimed at, will come to pass.

Even from the distance of a century and a borrowed tongue, the power of Bonifacio's words do not fail to move us, but more so if we were responding to the original Tagalog. The English translation cannot convey the texture, evoke the emotions, no matter how expertly handled; to do so, one would have to use the revolutionary idiom; not, for example, "What, then, must we do?" but Lenin's "What is to be done?" Words like "autochthonous," "concession," and "obfuscates" must be discarded.

We have to transport our imagination, recast our feelings, to the conditions of the nineteenth century Philippines, and, above all, react wholly to the exact emotional denotations of Bonifacio's prose.

There is a controversy in the translation of *"mga Tagalog"* into "Filipinos." Some historians consider this illegitimate, for Andres Bonifacio addressed "only" the Tagalogs. However, others tried to show that in other texts, "Filipinas" was the name given to the country, and that Filipinos in that period were understood officially as Spaniards born in the Philippines. Rizal and the propagandists tried to establish "Filipino" as the true identity of the colonized; still they would prefer Indios Bravos as their fighting identity. Dr. Milagros C. Guerrero, Ramon N. Villegas, and Emmanuel N. Encarnacion, refer to the asterisked footnote to the *Kartilya*, explaining that the word "tagalog" means "all those born in the archipelago; therefore, though visayan, ilokano, pampango, etc. they are tagalogs."

The Revolution, of course, was for all the native inhabitants of the "Philippine islands." If validated, the *Kartilya* footnote argues for the expanded notion of "Tagalog," thus dismissing charges of parochialism and Tagalog "imperialism." The Pampangos did not seem to mind, counting themselves among the original eight provinces to heed the Cry of Revolution. Nevertheless, non-Tagalog historians and chroniclers seem obsessed by the distinction, reflecting perhaps their own bias rather than that of the Katipunan.

But quite apart from the importance of the "Tagalog-Filipino" distinction from the scholarly point of view, there seems to be another motive for the emphasis. It is to show that Andres Bonifacio had a narrow view of Revolution, that he was "local" rather than "national," thus clearing the ground for the forces that sacrificed him to their "national vision."

Still, the importance of *Ang Dapat Mabatid*, its revolutionary power, is dramatized by its necessary place in the initiation of Katipunan members. They were asked three questions in the tradition of revolutionary "catechisms":

> *What was the condition of the country in early times?*
> *What is her condition today?*
> *What will be her condition in the future?*

The last question anticipates the famous revolutionary question: *What is to be done?*

The answers, of course, are not in the pile of brilliant protest literature but in the compact manifesto, *Ang Dapat Mabatid ng mga Tagalog*. Katipuneros got the message in this concise form just as many communists, apart from the leaders and theoreticians, got their Marxism from the *Communist Manifesto* instead of *Das Kapital*.

As the supreme revolutionist, Andres Bonifacio "distilled" all his readings and the totality of his experience into the forging of *Ang Dapat Mabatid ng mga Tagalog* as the irresistible summons to Revolution.

The Poet of the Revolution

By way of necessary digression: In his groundbreaking *Ang Panitikan ng Rebolusyon* (The Literature of the Revolution), the Tagalog poet, critic, and literary scholar, Virgilio Almario, teases me for being sparing, "stingy," in my recognition of Andres Bonifacio as a writer, let alone a poet. My guilt in this respect has more to do with distinction and emphasis without, however, any hint of diminution or dismissal of the hero's literary abilities.

My attitude is more complex than the literary critic's "canon," raised, as Almario observed, in the tradition of European literature. Love, whether of country, nature, or (more frequently) a person, can induce in the most inarticulate among us an outpouring of words that may or may not stand critical scrutiny. In the case of Bonifacio, his prose and verse can and do stand scrutiny, and it is quite right of Almario to show in a book-length essay that the "cultivated" commentators of Bonifacio's oeuvre are either wrong or simply precious.

But the very fact that the emotional ballast of Bonifacio's literary works is love of country readily suggests that his expressive motive was not artistic. A revolutionary need not be *just* a revolutionary (as an aristocratic Russian lady once said of Lenin), he could just as well be an artist, a doctor, a printer's devil besides. Mao Ze Dong, Ho Chi Minh, Samurais wrote poetry not necessarily with a desire to go down in history as poets. Writers and philosophers like Vaclav Havel get to be presidents, but there is something about our Asian revolutionists that goad them, at certain periods, to lyricism. (Poets moved to revolution are a different story). Nevertheless, Bonifacio could not be called a poet in the revolution but a revolutionary who poeticized the revolution. His vocation was revolution: the literary product was of and for the revolution. It was therefore in reference to his overriding passion, not his talent, which made me ask Almario whether Bonifacio was a writer.

Although the young Bonifacio attempted a Spanish poem, *Mi Abanico*, it is questionable whether he would have pursued a life in letters, albeit in our native language, if, for some reason, he never contemplated and made revolution. I believe, however, he would be like one of many friends in Tondo who, endowed with a love of language, would "indulge" in poetic expression once in a while. For Bonifacio, however, the poetry would be inconceivable without the revolutionary passion.

As for his prose, especially the gripping *Ang Dapat Mabatid ng mga Tagalog*, it is indeed a masterpiece of summation and persuasion. A sophisticated literary critic can apply to it the same techniques of classical rhetoric applied to Mark Anthony's oration before the bloodied corpse of Julius Caesar. There was intention in every sentence in Bonifacio's work, a wealth of symbolism, and persuasive power, but the aim was not to make the reader admire the piece of work but to move him to action. It had nothing to do with "recollection in tranquility." It was meant to disturb, to arouse, to stir to arms. The author would not have been content with an exegesis of the text. He would have found it either frivolous or evasive. It is a manifesto, a call to arms, intended for the occasion and not for posterity. It is rather the action that addresses itself to posterity.

Undoubtedly, the other poems, including the masterly translation of Rizal's *Mi Ultimo Adios* were not written at leisure or in the midst of calm, as literary exercises, but forged in the fire of revolution.

Andres Bonifacio turned poetry into revolution and revolution into poetry.

CHAPTER THREE

Revolution!

I t is one thing to make plans for revolution and quite another to launch it. The classic revolutions, the French and the Russian, broke out "spontaneously," without any pre-arranged signals; the outbreak of the Russian Revolution took Lenin by surprise, although he was quick to sense that the opportunity for the Bolsheviks had come. In the case of the Philippine Revolution, it had a designated time, although it was precipitated by circumstances.

The general sentiment in Antipolo on the third of May, 1896, as voiced by Cavite leaders Emilio Aguinaldo (*Magdalo*) and Santiago V. Alvarez (*Magdiwang*), was that the Katipunan needed more time to prepare for revolution. The immediate problem was the lack of arms. Andres Bonifacio, on the other hand, was apprehensive because the Spaniards were already informed about the secret society. Some suspects had already been arrested. In any case, what was paramount to Bonifacio was not arms (which they could capture from the enemy) but the will to fight.

Nevertheless, Andres Bonifacio was overruled. But to soften the blow of his rejection, it was proposed to consult Dr. Jose Rizal in Dapitan, a mission assigned to Dr. Pio Valenzuela, the ilustrado member of the Secret Chamber. The result of Dr. Valenzuela's consultation was not revealed to the other Katipunan leaders; it was naturally assumed that Rizal was at the very least cool to the idea. Unquestionably, the perception influenced many of the council leaders.

The respite proved to be a short and tragic one, even if in the interval, Katipunan membership continued to grow. Some Katipunan councils sponsored dances, beauty contests, picnics (who said that revolution was not a picnic?) for recruitment and initiation. Katipuneros organized outside Manila, making full use of a new conveyance: the bicycle. But on 18 July a quarrel over a two-peso wage increase led to the discovery of the Katipunan in the Manila printing shop of *Diario de Manila*, from which some of the typefaces for *Kalayaan* were procured by members, among them the foreman Apolonio de la Cruz, treasurer of the *Maghiganti* council in Tondo. In fact, all of the workers in the printing shop were Katipuneros; only the other foreman (in charge of tools and equipment), a certain Patiño, was not a "brother."

One day, the Spanish general manager of the shop by the name of Lafon, announced that there would be a two-peso increase for either de la Cruz or Patiño. Why he could not simply divide the increase between the two, giving them a total monthly wage of P19 each instead of just one getting P20, must be a clear case of sadism or favoritism (Patiño was supposedly his "protégé"). Anyway, he probably wanted to see a competition between de la Cruz and Patiño. In his revulsion for Patiño and desire to merit the additional two pesos for the Katipunan's coffers, Apolonio de la Cruz resorted to an anonymous poison letter against Patiño, who, until then, gave no hint that he knew what was going on with the Katipuneros in the shop. The vicious letter accused Patiño of stealing typefaces, paper, ink, and other materials and selling them. Confronted by Lafon about the poison letter, Patiño in turn confronted the workers, shouting, "I am not an evil man. No one can prove that I am either shameless or a thief. Now we shall know who is really evil!"

"Who among us are you referring to?" challenged the workers. There were heated words, but before the workers could mob Patiño, Lafon stepped out of his office and told all of them to go home. After ordering the guard to lock up, Lafon also left—only to return with a Spanish police lieutenant. They forcibly opened Apolonio de la Cruz's desk and there found incriminating evidence: rosters, oaths, and ledgers of the Maghiganti chapter of the Katipunan.

All this was seen by the guard, who immediately hailed a calesa, and after a brief stop at his house, sallied forth to inform his comrades about what had happened.

On the same night at ten, the police and civil guards arrested the implicated in their houses. By next morning, a Sunday, "there was a wailing of parents, kin, wives, and children of the arrested." Those who fell in the initial arrests were mercilessly tortured until some of them were forced to implicate both Katipuneros and non-Katipuneros alike, the innocent no less than the guilty.

In the provinces, the surveillance of suspects was tightened while the friars extracted more information from confessing women, although the friars, notably Mariano Gil of Tondo, insisted that they obtained damaging information outside of the confessional. The confessing women were, of course, merely bargaining for the safety of husbands, fathers, and brothers, proving the prudence of the Katipunan's admonitions to the women of the Katipuneros to stop going to confession.

On Wednesday, four days after the discovery in *Diario de Manila*, rumors circulated about the arrest and torture of Andres Bonifacio and other leaders, and that the Spaniards would henceforth apply the dreaded *juez de cuchillo*, the "judgment of the knife," sparing neither the old nor the very young, male or female. Both Katipuneros and non-Katipuneros begged mercy from the priests and the Spanish authorities, while others rallied to Bonifacio in Manila (later called the province of Rizal), when rumors about his arrest proved false.

Fray Mariano Gil, the parish priest of Tondo, supposedly the object of an assassination attempt by Bonifacio and Valenzuela, also claims his own discovery of the Katipunan. He dated this feat on 19 August 1896, when Patiño of *Diario de Manila* fame informed him of a plot "to kill you and all the Spaniards."

In the account of Katipunan leader Aguedo del Rosario, the priest also figured as the confessor of a *Cabesang* Simona of Barrio Bangkusay, whose curiosity was aroused by the number of visitors of Leon Magno, an ailing Katipunero. When the man died, so many unfamiliar faces turned up at the funeral, which was puzzling since Magno was not popular with his neighbors, as "he had never been more than a miserable *habanero* (a maker of Cuban-style cigars)." By keeping a watchful eye and keen ears, Simona, a member of the Venerable Third Order of Saint Francis, learned that the visitors and mourners were Katipuneros.

As she associated them with the dreaded Masons and filibusteros, she immediately informed Fray Mariano Gil of her discovery.

An interesting bit in del Rosario's recollections was the "reconstruction" of the Supreme Council in 1896 into "a ministry," creating the portfolios of State under Emilio Jacinto, War under Teodoro Plata, Justice under Briccio Pantas, Finance under Enrique Pacheco, and Interior under del Rosario. But these ministries "did not come into actual existence inasmuch as evil days had already come upon the Katipunan."

(This was to be alluded to nine months later at Tejeros when the Supremo asserted that the Revolution had a government and that it was the Katipunan. A supplementary note: an article in 8 February 1897 issue of *La Ilustracion Española y Americana* carried an engraved photograph of Andres Bonifacio with the caption *Titulado Presidente de la Republica Tagala*, while Emilio Aguinaldo was described as *generalissimo* of the army. It was also stated that Bonifacio had 60,000 troops under his command, 20,000 of them armed. Hence, the contention that Andres Bonifacio was actually the president of the first Philippine Republic.)

There must have been reprisals against betrayers and informers, but the only account of punishment is that of a certain Juana (Simona?), recounted by Sofronio Calderon in 1925. (Mariano Gil's account is dated 24 November 1896.)

On the night of 20 August, Salustiano Cruz met with Benito Concepcion, Santiago Reyes, Maximo Santos and Juan Tandang and abducted the woman. They then tied her upside down and cut her body in half, depositing half of it at the convent door and the other half on the steps of the church patio. Afterwards, they reported to Bonifacio in Balintawak what they had done.

This brutal act is nothing compared, however, to the atrocities committed by the Spanish authorities on those innocent as well as guilty of being Katipuneros.

But the Spaniards miscalculated the total effect of terrorism. As many as those who capitulated, thousands more, either out of desperation or disgust (convinced by now that there was no escaping the ruthlessness of the Spaniards) besieged the Katipunan centers. For days and nights, admissions and initiations went on.

It was also providential, or probably an indication of Spanish arrogance, that no spies penetrated the Katipunan councils. At the same time, the Katipuneros, old and new, and the wives they left behind, wanted to see the Supremo, reviling and cursing him when they could not. "Where is he? What has he done? He leads us to the brink of death and now he is hiding!" In the hour of their fear, need, and anger, their one single thought was to see the Supremo.

The Supremo had left town a few days before, leaving his wife, Gregoria de Jesus, in Kalookan, who learned from friends and relatives that she would also be arrested. She decided to go back to Manila in the dead of night, going by the rice fields direct to La Loma.

"I was treated like an apparition," Gregoria recalled years later, "for sad to say, from every house where I tried to get a little rest, I was driven away as if the people therein were frightened." But she learned afterwards that the occupants of the houses where she sought refuge were either severely punished or exiled. One of them was an uncle who died in exile. Her father and two brothers were also arrested.

At ten in the evening of 21 August, 1896, a Friday, the Katipuneros met in the house of Brother Vidal Akab in Kalookan. Among those in attendance, apart from a large group of followers, were Andres Bonifacio, Emilio Jacinto, Pio Valenzuela, Pantaleon Torres, Ariston de Jesus, Teodoro Plata, Jose Dizon, and Silverio Baltazar. Fearing that the Spanish troops might surprise them, Ramon Bernardo proposed that they proceed to the town of Kangkong.

In an hour, they started walking under the unrelenting rain, crossing muddy fields, their clothes drenched and their bodies shivering in the cold; everyone was exhausted and hungry. They reached the house of Brother Apolonio Samson where they were served rice and carabao meat.

Dawn the next day, Bonifacio was up and about and posting sentries at strategic points, giving them the signs and passwords for the day, and then called on Emilio Jacinto to write all the council presidents summoning them and their treasurers to Kangkong.

Besides the leaders, Andres Bonifacio had three hundred men equipped with bolos, spears, and daggers, a dozen revolvers, and a hunting rifle between them. Although cool at all times, he was nevertheless worried about the fate of the couriers, for they could fall into the hands of the Spaniards. Bonifacio's first concern in battle was for his men— he even took a bullet, a mere graze, that would have hit Emilio Jacinto.

El Supremo decided to move on again, this time to the house of Melchora Aquino, the famed *Tandang Sora*, in Sampalukan, Bahay-Toro. This was the third day since they met at the house of Vidal Akab. The grapevine brought them more Katipuneros as well as 100 bolos sent by Brother Apolonio Santos through Arcadio de Jesus.

On the fourth day, the Katipuneros numbered a thousand men, now joined by Briccio Pantas, Enrique Pacheco, Francisco Carreon, and Vicente Fernandez. It was here that the strategy for the attack on Manila on 29 August, a Saturday, was finalized. With the adjournment at noon, the revolutionaries shouted, "Long Live the Sons of the People!"

Tuesday, 25 August, a sentry announced the approach of the enemy. The Katipuneros faced them on the road between Kangkong and Bahay-Toro. There was a brief exchange of gunfire, after which the civil guards and the *carabinieros* withdrew. A fifteen-year-old boy was killed in the crossfire.

The next day, the 26th, the Katipuneros marched out of Sampalukan. With them as the Leader of Arms was Gregorio Tapalla of San Francisco de Malabon, Cavite, variously called *Laon* and *Old Leon*, a bandit leader who had escaped from jail. This old sot was killed in the first ambuscade of the Katipunan in Pasong Tamo. In the confusion, a suitcase containing the flag and money of the KKK was left behind. Old Leon's gang broke it open and stole the money. A barrage from the enemy cannon felled them. The Bago-Bantay Katipuneros, following on their heels, recovered the flag but kept silent about the incident, fearing that they would be asked about the money that the Old Leon gang stole. Old habits are not easy to break even in a noble and patriotic struggle.

In direct contrast was the behavior of Genaro de los Reyes, who was assigned by El Supremo to seek the aid of the Mandaluyong council. It took de los Reyes five hours to reach Mandaluyong on foot, where the

Makabuhay president, Laureano Gonzales, immediately formed an "aid committee." A baker by the name of Simeon gave 300 loaves of bread; two Chinese storeowners donated two packages of cigarettes, two packages of matches, five tins of sardines, and five pesos; Jose Reyes gave thirty pieces of clothing. He was also asked by Gonzales to help Genaro de los Reyes carry the items of succor back to the Bonifacio camp. But Genaro de los Reyes finally had to make it alone, since Jose Reyes turned pale from stomach cramps and could not go on with the journey.

It was now the 27th of August, Thursday. Despite his heavy load, de los Reyes walked as fast as he could, trying to beat the torrential rains. In San Juan del Monte, he chanced upon two Katipuneros, first Gregorio Bautista, who gave him five pesos, then a certain Torres, who gave twenty pesos and a telescope from Celestino Santos, president of the Marikina council. Near Krus ng Ligas, he sighted and evaded a detachment of civil guards and infantry. Reaching the Balara junction towards high noon, he encountered a group of hungry brothers, to whom he gave bread, sardines, and cigarettes before proceeding on his way to look for Bonifacio.

He then met with a farmer who feigned ignorance about the whereabouts of Bonifacio until he gave the Katipunan sign. "Come," the lookout said, laughing. "I will take you to them."

He was led to a small nipa hut in the thick of the woods where he found El Supremo, Dr. Pio Valenzuela, Emilio Jacinto, and twenty Katipuneros lunching on boiled bananas. A delighted Supremo stood up to meet and embrace the brave messenger. Everyone was beside himself over the food and other stuff that Genaro de los Reyes had brought. Indeed, in the early stages, the Katipuneros, from the top leaders to the humblest soldier, were often cold, ill-garbed, and hungry.

After a while, Bonifacio alerted his men for the climb to Tapusi hill where they could build a strong fortress against the enemy. However, Genaro de los Reyes pointed out that the Mandaluyong leadership wished them to come down instead because thousands needed Bonifacio for the preparations of 29 August, the agreed time for the uprising. Jacinto supported de los Reyes and convinced Bonifacio to come down to Mandaluyong. At this time, Agapito de Leon, secretary of the Marikina council, arrived to inquire whether the 29 August strike would push through at the designated hour of midnight.

Bonifacio's call to Revolution is dated 28 August—"Mountain of Liberty 28 August in the Year of the Lord 1896."

> *Presidents, brothers, you are called upon…to gather all our brothers and inform them that at midnight Saturday we shall start the Revolution in our respective towns and those who will strike at Manila will come from Balara, proceed to Ugong hill and cross Guadalupe (San Pedro, Makati) and strike the civil guards in Santa Ana. Any brother who disagrees with this noble purpose will be considered a traitor and be numbered among the enemy, while those who are truly sick will be cared for according to our rules.*

This was almost certainly a mere reminder, for as early as 23 August, many people already knew that the Revolution would begin on the 29th. This early knowledge gave heart to all of those who feared for their lives and the lives of their loved ones. They were awaiting the day of redemption. Arms remained a problem but they were determined to fight nonetheless. Historians will later say that the Katipunan was not a fighting force; still, they were ready to fight. The courage and the nobility of that resolution was the heart of the Revolution.

As they proceeded to Mandaluyong, the Katipuneros were again drenched by heavy rains. While waiting out the downpour in the warehouse of Kabesang Claro, they spotted an emaciated horse, butchered it and boiled the edible flesh without salt, eating it with banana and the few remaining loaves of bread. They resumed their trek when the rain had abated, but Dr. Valenzuela, fatigued and suffering from the cold, begged to be left behind. He was escorted back by a Katipunero to Malanday, Marikina. Later on, there were rumors that he had been captured by the Spaniards and tortured, a story that was later proved false to the eternal shame of Pio Valenzuela.

The truth was three days after the outbreak of the revolution, Pio Valenzuela surrendered himself to the Spaniards to avail of the amnesty offered by Governor General Ramon Blanco. (The amnesty was extended to 21 September 1896, but Valenzuela was already there on the 1st of September, two days before the expiration of the original amnesty deadline.) He was interrogated for a long period by the Spaniards, during which he implicated many people, including the unfortunate Francisco Roxas, all of whom were executed. He absolved Dr. Jose Rizal of all involvement with either the Katipunan or the Revolution, and laid all the blame on Andres Bonifacio. He went so far as to accuse Bonifacio, depicting him a s a murderous man, of having forced him to join the Katipunan at gunpoint, and succeeded in convincing the Spaniards that he was just "small fry" in the KKK, having no Pacto de Sangre mark on his wrist, although he boasted in his memoirs that he was the third member of the Secret Chamber and was even part of the plot to assassinate Fr. Mariano Gil. We shall never understand why the Spaniards, so merciless with so many innocent others, did not execute him. A tempting thought is that they considered the information he gave as valuable enough to earn him his life and freedom. Even so, his memoirs about some aspects of the Katipunan are reliable insofar as they are corroborated by others.

Interestingly, there are three Pios in the life and death of Andres Bonifacio: Pio Pi, the priest who figured in the aborted negotiations with Emilio Aguinaldo; Pio del Pilar, whom Aguinaldo identified as one of the generals who convinced him to have Bonifacio killed; and Pio Valenzuela.

To resume our story, at ten o'clock on the night of 27 August, other Katipunan leaders arrived at the house of Brother Gregorio de la Cruz. It was decided to call a final meeting in Mandaluyong. Our chronicler, Aguedo del Rosario, could not resist noting that it was in the house of de la Cruz that the Supremo had his first good meal in seven days, while the rest also had warm but ill-fitting clothes and shoes.

At three o'clock the next morning, 28 August, the Supremo again assigned Genaro de los Reyes to check the preparations in Santulan while he, Bonifacio, would repair to Balacbac in the house of Romualdo Vicencio. He reminded the Marikina Katipuneros to stick close to their headquarters so that they could readily receive all communications.

By eight that morning, Santulan was already astir with the summons to Revolution. There were more enlistments to the Katipunan, with many new members donating a peso each. By two in the afternoon, the chapter treasurer had collected a hundred fifty pesos. As for inventory of arms, there were fifteen Remington guns and a rifle. Bonifacio received all the money at four o'clock in the afternoon. This was also the time recorded by Santiago V. Alvarez for the writing of the Proclamation, which could only mean that the news about the Revolution had reached the other towns by word of mouth.

The 28th of August was a day of activity and excitement, perhaps even euphoria, for after a whole week of tension and anxiety—not to mention the months of depredation, the sons of the People were finally going to strike back at their oppressors. Informed by Laureano Gonzales that the enemy had set up a small encampment at the Mandaluyong side of the Pasig River and that another cannon had been installed on the San Juan del Monte riverbank opposite the water reservoir where an artillery detachment had taken position, the Katipuneros eagerly awaited the battle that was to come.

It was now 29 August. While the Katipuneros prepared for the hour of Revolution, they received the sad news (later proved untrue as previously stated) that Dr. Pio Valenzuela was being tortured inside the parish house of the Catholic church in San Mateo. But the Revolution could not be detained by grief over their first prominent "casualty." Genaro de los Reyes was sent out again to check the availability of arms among the Mandaluyong councils, where he found one rifle and one Remington gun, and only bolos, daggers, and spears in one; bladed weapons and two Remingtons in another, and only one firelock aside from bladed weapons in the third. Concentrating on procuring additional firearms from the enemy, Genaro was rewarded by Katipunero Tomas Arienda Jose who succeeded in smuggling out of the Mandaluyong friar estate three guns and some ammunition, while Juan Capulco procured a firelock, two Remingtons, one rifle, and bullets.

At five that afternoon, Andres Bonifacio had more than 500 men "in arms" in the village Hagdang Bato in Mandaluyong, stopping by the house of Brother Felix Sanchez. Mandaluyong had seventeen chapters under Laureano Gonzales' Makabuhay Council. All the chapters prepared food for their comrades in the homes of Simeon Borja, a bakery owner; Pascual Francisco, a former municipal captain, and Brother Tranquilino Mendiola. By seven that night, there were more than a thousand Katipuneros in Hagdang Bato. The Supremo distributed the guns to the few who knew how to handle them. At the same time, he ordered Brother Buenaventura Domingo, chairman of the Tala Chapter, to keep a close watch on the Mandaluyong parish house to see to it that the cura did not escape.

The Mandaluyong Katipunan had infiltrated the local police force, so that five *cuadrilleros* (squad leaders), Sgt. Felix Sanchez, chairman of *Matunog* chapter; Froilan Tatko, Cirilo (alias *Butas*), Luciano Benito (alias *Mulawin*), and Fermin (alias *Matanda*), led by Lt. Leon Bautista, chairman of the *Malanday* chapter, were assigned to lure the civil guards out of the *presidencia* town hall. Failing at this, they asked the Supremo's permission to storm the town hall. Giving his permission, Bonifacio coordinated the movements of several chapters and after giving instructions, the Katipuneros shouted "Long Live the Sons of the People!" and as far as our chronicler was concerned, this was the first battle cry of the Katipunan, coinciding with the pealing of church bells at nine in the evening of 29 August 1896. The pealing over, El Supremo cried out, "Advance!"

It was three hours before the hour of midnight of 29 August 1896, the revolutionary hour to be signaled by balloons in the air and cannon fire from Manila, signifying that the Katipunan had struck at the heart of tyranny. An hour later, *Apoy* (Artemio Ricarte), *Labong* (Mariano Trias) and their men began the vigil of the Revolution in Cavite.

But at eleven that night, after an encounter with the enemy in Mandaluyong, Bonifacio and his men had another clash in San Juan del Monte. They killed two Spanish soldiers and captured some arms. After this victory, they were joined by 300 Katipuneros from Santulan under the command of Valentin Cruz. Reinforced, the Supremo looked at this timepiece: it was four o'clock in the morning ... 30 August!

The hour was lost. What else was lost? The Katipunan in the provinces struck on their own. Artemio Ricarte was the first to strike in Malabon (now General Trias) in the morning, followed by Alvarez in the afternoon at Noveleta.

The Katipuneros in Manila and environs are praised by some historians for their valor, not for their military skills. Perhaps, these critics have some secret strategy by which bolos, daggers, bamboo lances, and a few guns can overwhelm trained troops, not to mention cavalry, armed with rifles, guns, and cannons? Nevertheless, General Echaluce would testify that "in the initial stages of the rebellion, when the purpose of the insurgents became clear, the panic in Manila was indescribable."

As for the initial impregnability of Cavite, he called it "a glaring error" to blame him for not attacking Cavite. "In the first place it was my duty not to abandon the city of Manila as I was its military governor. A military governor cannot absent himself from his appointed position under the law, except in case of illness, and no less when the position is surrounded or almost surrounded, as Manila was."

An opportunity for a dramatic strike was lost when the midnight of 29 August came and went. The simultaneous strikes in the eight provinces would have immediately struck terror, rather than just panic, in the hearts of the Spaniards.

Gen. Echaluce still was optimistic:

> *The insurrection is Tagalog. There was not, when I left, a single person from any other province mixed up in it. The chief directors, or most of them, have been arrested. The bands in Nueva Ecija, Pampanga, Bulacan and Batangas were unorganized when I left.*
>
> *The principal centers of direction are in Manila and its chiefs are the most wealthy half-castes.*
>
> *If some native soldiers have gone over the rebels with their arms it is understandable when we consider what the Filipino is. Without Spanish leaders, and finding themselves corralled and some of them sacrificed, the rest is self-explanatory; in face of superior numbers and possessed with a natural panic, without initiative and the great stimulant of patriotism (Spanish patriotism?), they did what they did without being imbued with the real spirit of revolt. (!)*

The truth was the "unpatriotic" Filipino soldiers were infected by the spirit of the Katipunan.

The general did not "concede importance at the present time to the bands which, according to recent telegrams, have appeared in Bataan and Zambales."

"I believe that as long as the revolt does not spread into the Visayas, although it is serious, it will not be difficult to dominate it."

Generals are often wrong about revolutions, when they are fighting not armies but an aroused people.

After the dramatic events of the August week in 1896, Andres Bonifacio "disappeared." He was nowhere to be found, which was not surprising, since the Spanish authorities could not find him either. He was actually lodged, along with Emilio Jacinto, in the house of Isabelo Donato y Aguilar on 160 Soler. A rich man, Donato identified himself with the working class and believed in Bonifacio's ideals; he also did intelligence work for the Supremo. His father, a Freemason, was arrested and tortured in Fort Santiago; later on his entire property in Aranque, consisting of a row of commercial and apartment houses, was burned by Filipino forces trying to delay the advance of Americans. Bonifacio finally settled in a house at 116 Lavezares before he departed to meet his destiny in Cavite.

Though in hiding, Bonifacio exercised his command of the revolution, as evidenced by the manifesto *Katipunan Mararahas Ng Mga Anak ng Bayan* (Audacious Association of the Sons of the People), in which the ideas of the *Ang Dapat Mabatid Ng Mga Tagalog* were repeated in the heat of battle, adding forcefully "the burning of children" to the rape of women and the sufferings of the aged. Bonifacio wrote to his comrades:

> *The valor that you have manifested in the fight against the Spanish army since the commencement of the revolution eminently proves that you are not disheartened by the signs of military preparations and the imminent attack by Polavieja's army which, in so short at time, has already shown sheer cowardice and a slave's meanness of character in torturing and killing so many Filipino non-combatants.*

He reminded them that those who would die would leave a legacy to the country, the race and to their progeny: "Your death will infuse life into our country and will serve as a sweet remembrance to your sisters and brothers who will be left behind."

That he was not, as his later detractors would hold, a cruel and barbarous man, the ending of the manifesto, which had the tone of command, clearly belies:

> *In all this, and in order that the sacredness and honor of our country be made complete, in order that that the whole world might witness the nobility of our character, let us not emulate our enemy in this detestable conduct of war, let us not go to battle merely in the interest of killing, but rather in defense of the liberty of our country, and thus fighting cry out at the top of our voices: Mabuhay! LONG LIVE THE SOVEREIGN PEOPLE OF THE PHILIPPINES!*

The concluding cry was the interpolation of Teodoro Agoncillo and S. V. Espitola to the Tagalog *Mabuhay Ang Haring Bayang Katagalugan*, literally "Long Live the Sovereign *Tagalog* Country." Was Andres Bonifacio being exclusivist, or was he just making a distinction between the name that the Spaniards gave to the Philippines and the land he claimed for all his countrymen? The resolution to this question lies in the fact that the liberty he fought for was not just for the Tagalogs.

Nevertheless, this non-issue became an issue for those who would limit the hero's vision to Manila and environs, despite the fact that the Cry of Balintawak was the cry of an entire people rising in arms against centuries-old enslavement. A resounding cry, for as 1896 ended, the Revolution had spread to Ilocano Zambales and Pangasinan, Bicolano Camarines Sur and Albay, and Visayan Iloilo, Cebu, and Negros. Indio soldiers deserted their Spanish regiments and joined the Katipunan, who welcomed them not only from strength of blood but also for their military experience. There was, of course, no more time for inductions and rituals: all that was required was the willingness to fight the common enemy. And yet it was the spirit of the Katipunan and its founder that pervaded the revolutionary ranks.

The spirit was too strong for Spanish arms. It was to be conquered by something else.

Cry of Balintawak

There is still a raging controversy over the date and place of the *Cry* heard for a century and a year. The official date and place, based on the historian Teodoro Agoncillo's account, is 23 August 1896 in Pugad Lawin. However, to a new breed of historians, among them Dr. Milagros C. Guerrero, Ramon N. Villegas and Emmanuel N. Encarnacion, the official date and place is unverifiable outside of Valenzuela's muddled account. Instead, 24 August 1896 is proposed, and at the barn of Tandang Sora (Melchora Aquino) in Gulod, now barangay Banlat, Quezon City.

A table published in *Sulyap Kultura*, citing different sources, suggests "what really happened."

On 20 August (Manuel Artigas based on Jose Turiano Santiago, 1911), "cries of *Mueron los Easpañoles* (Death to the Spaniards!) and *Viva la Republica Filipina* are heard after a lengthy Katipunan meeting."

On 22 August (Santiago Alvarez, in *Sampaguita*, 1927-28), "Andres Bonifacio asks Emilio Jacinto to summon the chapter heads and treasurers of the Katipunan Councils to a meeting at Kangkong."

On 23 August (Reparaz, in *La Ilustracion Española y Americana*), "Andres Bonifacio calls a meeting of the Katipunan Supreme Council but fails to gather a quorum," and (Cecilia Manzano, 1989) "Katipunan and Spanish forces clash in Kangkong," and (Artemio Ricarte, 1927): "A gathering called by Bonifacio in Balintawak, a town of Kalookan, is discovered by the Civil Guard who fired at the people, killing a number of them, the rest escaping to the forest." This led to the Battle of Pinaglabanan.

Sofronio Calderon (1925) says that the "revolt was to have begun on 29 August 1896," but the time was not set; however, the site was Kangkong and not Pugad Lawin, the signal to be made by the *remontado* (bandit) Laon.

Sinforoso San Pedro (1925) tells of a Chinese spy being caught on 23 August and taken for interrogation to Apolonio Samson's house in Kangkong, the same place maintained by Guillermo Masangkay.

The next day, 23 August, the famous meeting was held in Kangkong. After Bonifacio told the throng everything that had happened and about the danger threatening them, it was moved that the revolt begin. Plata, Briccio Pantas, and Valenzuela objected. But when the matter was put to a vote, the majority agreed to revolt.

Bonifacio then stood in front of the people and asked once more.if they would go through with the revolt, and almost all voiced their assent. Those gathered declared their autonomy and freedom from Spain, and as a symbol of their determination tore their cedulas (poll tax receipts) to pieces, for these were symbols of slavery as anyone who did not have a cedula and did not pay the tax was punished and imprisoned.

With tears of joy in their eyes, the people shouted, "We are free from slavery!" and "Long Live the Tagalogs!"

Four other accounts agree on 24 August as the day of mobilization and establishment of Bonifacio's "new government" in Pasong Tamo, identified as the house of Matandang or Tandang Sora, Melchora Aquino. A Civil Guard detachment headed by a Lt. Ros encounters the 2000-strong rebels and withdraws; while the Spanish historian Sastron states that the rebels started arming themselves at noon of 25 August. The decision to start the revolution on 29 August was made there.

In Santiago Alvarez's account, the Supreme Council meeting took place in Tandang Sora's barn in sitio Gulod, Barrio Banlat, Kalookan, during which these were agreed upon: the Katipunan would start the Revolution on the midnight of 29 August, a Saturday; Aguedo del Rosario, Vicente Fernandez, Ramon Bernardo, and Gregorio Coronel were appointed Brigadiers-General with the complete freedom to select their troop leaders; they would also formulate the tactics for breaking into Manila, with General del Rosario passing at the back of Bilibid, General Coronel through Tondo, General Fernandez through San Marcelino, General Bernardo through the Rotonda, all converging in Manila.

These varying versions were resolved in favor of 24 August at Balintawak instead of Pugad Lawin, which apparently does not exist in the municipal records, according to Sofronio Calderon, a writer and linguist. Three references were provided.

First, the Tagalog and Spanish texts of the *Biyak na Bato* Constitution attest that the separation of the Philippines from the Spanish monarchy, *constituting an independent state and with a proper sovereign government*, named the Republic of the Philippines, was the end pursued through "the present hostilities" initiated on 24 August 1896. (This document was signed a year and a half after the event by over fifty Katipunan members, among them Emilio Aguinaldo, Artemio Ricarte, and Valentin Diaz.)

Second, 1928 and 1930 photographs of surveys with several Katipunan officers published in *La Opinion*, claiming that the Cry took place on the 24th.

Third, Emilio Aguinaldo's memoirs (*Mga Guinita ng Himagsikan*), citing two letters from Andres Bonifacio dated 22 and 24 August. In part, Aguinaldo wrote: "Our representation arrived safely at his destination and also returned unharmed, *bearing a letter from the Supremo dated 24 August*. It contained no orders but the *shocking* announcement that the Katipunan would attack Manila at night on Saturday, 29 August, the signal for which would be the putting out of the lamps in Luneta. He added that many of his comrades had been captured and killed by the Civil Guard and Veterans in Gulod." (Italics given)

This places the site in Balintawak, a famous town near another, which is Kalookan. In any case, the consensus among the academe is that the famous Cry was made in the jurisdiction of Balintawak.

The conclusion, perhaps, is to scrap Pugad Lawin in spite of its romantic aura and to make Balintawak and 24 August official. But if, as Aguinaldo attests, he received Bonifacio's letter dated 24 August, the event could have transpired a few hours to a day before the letter was dispatched by courier. Perhaps, the better way, in this era of "weeks," is to declare August 23 to 29 "The Week of the Cry" giving Pugad Lawin the benefit of a doubt, as part of Balintawak.

But this is a matter to be settled by scholars and historians, who often disagree on many matters of fact and opinion.

All the same, the significant element in these events is the presence of Andres Bonifacio, leading the Katipuneros through "hills and valleys," as it were, to mount the first anti-colonialist revolution in Asia.

CHAPTER FOUR

The Crisis of the Hero

The first time Andres Bonifacio visited Cavite, he lost his house. The second time, he lost his life.

On his first visit, he was accompanied by the members of the Secret Chamber, Dr. Pio Valenzuela and Emilio Jacinto, and Pantaleon Torres. Their mission on that April morning in 1896 was to organize the Magdiwang Council in Noveleta.

It was Good Friday, a "Katipunan day," for the society always timed its activities on holidays. The party then proceeded to Kawit as secret guests of Emilio Aguinaldo, his cousin Baldomero and Candido Tirona, for the pacto de sangre initiation of new members. The oaths were still being administered at eight o'clock in the evening when people started shouting, "Fire! Fire in Manila!" Gazing at the horizon, Andres Bonifacio had the premonition that his house had burned down. Indeed, two days later, Bonifacio confirmed it to his host and escort at Noveleta, Santiago V. Alvarez.

Many important documents and Katipunan stuff were lost for all time, including the ones that his wife, Gregoria de Jesus, carried in her body whenever she had to leave the house. If Bonifacio had any memorabilia, these too were lost forever.

On the same day that Alvarez received the Supremo's letter, he was visited by Baldomero Aguinaldo who discussed the leadership of the Katipunan in Kawit. Alvarez said the Aguinaldos could establish a municipal chapter but not a *Sanggunian* (Council), for this needed the sanction of the Supremo. Nevertheless, the Magdalo Council was established in Kawit with Baldomero Aguinaldo as president. This was the first indication of the independent-mindedness of the Aguinaldos and the differences between the Magdiwang and the Magdalo councils.

Bonifacio's second visit was in response to the Magdiwang Council's persistent invitation to see for himself the progress of the Revolution in Cavite. Twice before, he considered it unwise for all the leaders to be gathered in one province: one concentrated attack by the Spanish forces could decimate the leadership. Bonifacio learned his lesson in August when the Spanish forces were concentrated in Manila. When he finally relented and succumbed to the Magdiwang's appeals, he made it clear that he would not linger, much less involve himself in the affairs of the Katipunan of Cavite, proud as he was of the successes of his brothers there.

In this spirit, he arrived in Imus in the afternoon of 17 December 1896, where he stayed in the house of Juan Castañeda. The next morning he was visited by Emilio and Baldomero Aguinaldo, Daniel Tirona, and others. Later on, Esteban San Juan extended the warm greetings of the Magdiwang Council. Bonifacio proceeded to Noveleta, where he was jubilantly received with a band, banners, and fireworks as the people shouted, "Long Live the Supremo," to which the Supremo responded with, "Long Live the Motherland!"

Everything went well for the Supremo until the day after Christmas, when rumors circulated in the towns of Cavite that the Manila Katipuneros no longer trusted the Supremo because he was under the pay of the friars to "create trouble," that he absconded with Katipunan money, that he had a beautiful sister under the sway of a Spanish priest in Tondo.

Bonifacio was also faulted for taking on the title of Supremo, for only God could be called such, and in total disregard of the fact that that title was generally used only in reference to the "President." (All council leaders were called president, and the title "Supremo" simply signified that he was the leader of the Supreme Council.) Capping the rumors were leaflets impugning the Supremo as an atheist (being a freemason, as many Katipunan leaders were), poorly educated, a German agent, and a hireling of the friars. The suspected author of these leaflets was Daniel Tirona, secretary of war of the Magdalo. When the Supremo confronted him in the house of Col. Santos Nocon, Tirona showed defiance in the same breath that he denied Bonifacio's accusation. The Supremo took out his revolver; but for the intervention of the women, Tirona's blood would have tainted the hands of Andres Bonifacio.

This was the second time that Bonifacio drew his revolver. The first time was at the outbreak of the Revolution when a Katipunan officer failed to prevent the escape of a friar. The third time would occur in Tejeros, again provoked by Tirona, foiled this time by Artemio Ricarte. There was also an account of an aborted duel between Andres and Ciriaco Bonifacio on one side, and Emilio and Baldomero Aguinaldo on the other, on 10 January 1897. Alvarez recounted that he prevented what would have been another shameful episode in the history of the Revolution. As he only came around when the duel was about to take place, Alvarez did not mention its immediate cause. In any case, this established that there was already bad blood between the Supremo and his erstwhile Captain in Cavite long before the gathering at Tejeros in March.

Whatever the personal reason for the bad blood, it undoubtedly had something to do with the rivalry between the Magdiwang and Magdalo. Although Bonifacio vowed not to intervene in their affairs, it was nonetheless clear to the Magdalo that he was partial towards the Magdiwang. It is not hard to see why: the Magdiwang recognized his authority, while the Magdalo did not. He had tried to assert his authority once during the first days of his visit but the Magdalo chiefs just ignored him.

Two other incidents in December 1896 should have alerted the Supremo to his unrecognized authority, quite apart from the scandalous rumors and libelous leaflets circulated against him.

The first occurred on the 29th of December at the liberated friar estate in Imus. Upon the invitation of Magdalo, the Magdiwang agreed to a unification meeting. A legislative body, headed by the Supremo, was elected to draft a constitution. But the proceedings were interrupted by the arrival of Paciano Rizal with a message from his brother saying that he would not countenance a rescue that involved more than one man. It was therefore useless for the Magdiwang to proceed with its plan to send troops to rescue him from his executioners. After listening to Paciano, the Supremo charged Baldomero Aguinaldo with the writing of the minutes, but the latter asked for a few days since so much time had been lost in listening to Rizal's elder brother. That was the last time he heard of the Imus agreement.

The Supremo must have sensed something amiss, for in a letter to President Mainam (Mariano, father of Apoy, Santiago Alvarez) dated 2 January 1897, he asked for an immediate meeting, ... "for we must talk privately about the incident that happened to me in the Magdalo Council and for you to explain to me how they were organized."

The second incident occurred during a visit made to the Supremo by Edilberto Evangelisto, fresh from his engineering studies in Belgium. He presented a draft constitution for a revolutionary government. (He must have heard of the meeting in Imus and could have been an agent of Aguinaldo.) But the Supremo recognized his draft as a copy of the "Real Orden" authored by Matira, the Spanish Minister of Ultramar. Stung, Evangelista went to Aguinaldo. In his memoirs, Aguinaldo quoted Evangelista as saying:

> *Let us not think that the Revolution is an affair of the* Katipunan *alone, instead of a struggle expressing the true sentiments of an entire nation. While still a student in Europe I already wished for a Revolution, and yet I was not a* Katipunero.

A more suspicious individual would have been more circumspect about the good faith of the Magdalo, but the Supremo, with his small contingent of twenty men, came for a meeting with the Magdalo on 22 March 1897 at the Tejeros friar estate in San Francisco de Malabon. This set the stage for the crisis in the hero's life.

All accounts show that the Supremo had been misled about the true purpose of the Magdalo-Magdiwang meeting. It was not, after all, to discuss how best to wage the revolutionary war against Spain, but to organize a revolutionary government to direct it.

The Magdiwang war secretary, Ariston Villanueva, had an intimation of what was going to happen, so he advised Santiago V. Alvarez to have armed soldiers on the alert.

Indeed, armed fighting among the revolutionaries could have occurred with the altercation between Antonio Montenegro and Alvarez. Severino de las Alas had proposed the organization of a revolutionary government, to which the Supremo replied that there was already a government under the Katipunan. Seconding de las Alas, Montenegro said that without a government proposed by de las Alas, they, the revolutionaries, would be no better than outlaws (*tulisan*), provoking Alvarez to challenge him to recapture towns lost to the Spaniards before he thought of putting up his own kind of government. Concluding his impassioned reply, Alvarez proposed to arrest Montenegro. According to Alvarez himself, Rizal's widow and sister, Josephine Bracken and Trinidad, intervened to pacify he combative Katipuneros.

The presiding officer, Jacinto Lumberas, yielded the chair to the Supremo. In what could only be regarded as a gesture of solidarity and nobility, the Supremo agreed to the beheading of the Katipunan (for that was the precise implication of establishing a revolutionary government) and the election of officials of a revolutionary government. However, he reminded everyone to respect the will of the majority.

What happened afterwards has been recounted to the point of weariness by Ricarte, Alvarez, and Masangkay, and repeated through the years by historians Teodoro A. Agoncillo and others. The Supremo was not elected President of the Revolutionary Government. He lost nomination after nomination until he was elected Secretary of the Interior. At this point, the ubiquitous Daniel Tirona stood to oppose the Supremo's election, saying that he was not qualified for such a powerful post. Humiliated and insulted for the second time by the same person, Bonifacio pulled out his revolver, but Tirona had disappeared in the crowd even before Ricarte intervened.

Saying that he did not recognize the validity of the proceedings, Andres Bonifacio, the Supremo of the Katipunan and the father of the Revolution, pronounced the death sentence.

It is convenient now to claim that the rejected Supremo could have saved his own life if he had not initiated the Acta de Tejeros and the Naic Military Agreement, since these created another "center" for the Revolution. Others say that he should have immediately left Cavite and joined either Emilio Jacinto in Laguna or other comrades in Nueva Ecija. Maybe he had counted on the support of the Magdiwang, except that around that time both the Magdiwang and the Magdalo were beleaguered by the Spanish forces.

In any case, the Spaniards' counter-attack did not exactly make it easy for a quick march. Nevertheless, he did write to Mariano Alvarez, leader of the Magdiwang and father of Santiago, to request for food and loyal soldiers of the Motherland, "as fulfillment of your promise to assist me in my speedy departure (from Cavite)."

The Supremo also wrote to Emilio Jacinto (24 April 1897) his appreciation of the events in Tejeros:

> ... *As to the convention held on the 22nd of last month, the cause of it was that Captain Emilio Aguinaldo had received letters from a Jesuit and a Spaniard, Pio Pi and Rafael Comenge by name. These letters state that they will grant us the most ample pardon, and if not, they ask for a conference in order that we might tell them what we want. Both letters were endorsed by the Imus people to the* Magdiwang *chiefs, with a list of conditions for the Spaniards, in order that an agreement might be arrived at. The* Magdiwang *people did not agree, for the reason that I was absent from Tanway, at Look (Batangas), in those days; besides they denied representation to the Jesuit and Comenge, who lacked authority* ad hoc *for this matter.*
>
> *When the Imus people received the reply of the* Magdiwang, *Captain Emilio wrote secretly to the chiefs of the* pueblos *under the jurisdiction of* Magdiwang *concerning the compromise he wished to make with the Spaniards. When the President of* Magdiwang *learned this, he immediately called a convention of the people and sent for me to Look, and the convention referred to was held. In view of my explanation regarding the inadvisability of such a compromise with the Spaniards, all the persons present there were of the opinion that the war should continue.*
>
> *The majority of the convention determined to organize a government but I gave them to understand that this could not be, on account of the absence of the representatives of other districts, aside from an agreement having already been adopted at the convention in Imus; that all this annulled the majority, because in view of the present critical situation of these* pueblos,

there was no time to wait for representatives from other places, and the Imus convention lacked validity, on account of the alleged absence of a minute record. Nevertheless I assured those present that I would respect the manifest will of the people governed in the election of officers.

When the election was held, there were elected, as President of the Republic, Don Emilio Aguinaldo; Vice-President, Don Mariano Trias; General-in-chief, Don Artemio Ricarte; Director of War, Don Emilio R. de Dios. This was all by acclamation, as it was night. I was elected Director of the Interior, also by acclamation, and was cheered by all, the same as the others who had been elected; but when the cheering was over and they were about to elect a Director of Finance, Don Daniel Tirona said that there were voices proclaiming Don Jose del Rosario as Director of Interior; at once he insinuated that since the position of Director of Interior was a most exacting one, a learned man must be selected, and this he said after stating that it was not his intention to offend me. I forthwith replied that learned men were required for all the other offices also, and asked him whom of those elected he could point out to me as being a learned man. Nevertheless he shouted: 'Acclaim as Director of Interior Jose del Rosario, the lawyer!' Nobody responded to his proposal in the four times that he shouted it, except a few, who acclaimed me instead. In view of the turmoil, the President of Magdiwang *declared that this was not a convention of gentlemen and that everything done there lacked validity.*

I also said that if the manifest will of the people was not complied with, I would not recognize any of the chiefs elected, and if I did not recognize them they would not be recognized by our people there, either. Don Artemio Ricarte, the General-elect, also said at that meeting that his election was due to bad practices.

The Imus people met the next day at the Tanza convent and there they compelled the officers-elect to take the oath, one by one, as you can see by the attached document by Don Artemio Ricarte.

The Magdiwang *people, particularly those from Malabon, objected (to what happened) and called Captain Emilio Aguinaldo and Daniel Tirona to a meeting to demand their resignations. Hence it was necessary to issue a circular throughout the* pueblos *saying that his (Aguinaldo's) election was null and void, and that matters between* Magdiwang *and* Magdalo *remained as it was before.*

I and our men, totaling 20 armed with Remington rifles, and about 20 with muzzle-loaders, left for the barrio of Halang (Limbon) of the pueblo *of Indang. We also had with us bolomen numbering 1,000, as we only await what you and Don Antonino Guevarra will decide, in accordance with the agreement between Guevarra and myself.*

As for the arms for which we are waiting, it seems that we cannot expect anything because Jocson's letter asks for 20,000 pesos, and the money collected here has nearly been used up by the chiefs for the needs of the war.

You will receive herewith a copy of the revolutionary Manifesto *that we are going to publish. It is in English, too, but as it is rather long, I entrust you to fix it ... The cipher code for letters to Hong Kong is also enclosed. You must keep this secret from Mamerto Natividad.*

The District of Batangas has organized a provincial government which is placed under my orders, according to the four letters I have received. I sent 20 riflemen and 25 Balara bolomen to help them. Luciano also went there with several riflemen to help in the general attack they are going to make there on 8 pueblos *at the same time.*

As to the report of Procopio's (Bonifacio's brother), there is not truth in it, but he was in serious danger.

I also received news here that you had been killed by the carabineers because you had given a bad order; but as this came form Imus, I did not believe it and considered it one of the tricks of the crowd.

As to the collection of money, I believe we need not beg, but the best thing to do is try to enter the pueblos *and solicit or take it from the rich. Brother M. Nakpil wrote me, asking whether he was to deliver the money he collected, four hundred pesos, to Mamerto Natividad. Do not permit this because the man (Natividad) is not loyal to us; he is very thick with the* Magdalo *people.*

A piece of news that turns the stomach is that of the perfidy committed by the Magdalo *officers who applied for pardon or went over to the Spaniards. These are Daniel Tirona (again!), Minister of War; Jose del Rosario, Minister of Interior; Jose Cailles (actually Juan), Lieutenant-General; and nearly all the Tanza people, even the parish priest there, all henchmen of Captain Emilio's. For this reason, many people strongly suspect that they work so hard to get control of the government in order to put down the whole Revolution.*

Last week I ordered one of Captain Emilio's ministers bound, because he was caught, as he was about to escape with two Spanish prisoners and a lady. One of these Spaniards told the truth, that they were going to make their escape. He was tried by a military commission, but the usual thing happened: reciprocity and favoritism. But the cases against the minister mentioned, Sr. Cayetano Topacio, and the Spaniards remained in my possession. This is one of the reasons we desire to leave here, because our life is in danger not only from the Spanish enemy, but still more from the leaders here, the majority of whom are bad.

On 24 April 1897, the Supremo was eager to leave Cavite for the Silangan hills in San Mateo, Morong. He and his contingent, most of whom were bolomen, were now temporarily in Limbon, Indang. His letter to Jacinto mentioned no shortage of food. But the story went around that he had ordered his men to solicit contributions, and when they were refused, he gave orders to burn the town and spare no one. This was reported to Aguinaldo in Naic.

Three days after he had written to Jacinto, Andres Bonifacio, founder of the Katipunan and father of the Revolution, was arrested, along with his brother Ciriaco, by Colonel Agapito Bonzon, Felix Topacio, and Jose Ignacio Pawa upon orders of President Emilio Aguinaldo. At the time, the Supremo had already decided to march out the next morning to join Emilio Jacinto and Julio Nakpil in San Mateo. This was also the recollection of Lieutenant Colonel Nicomedes Carreon.

Shots were fired. Ciriaco fell dead. Procopio was hurt and Andres Bonifacio was wounded on the left arm. Pawa stabbed him on the neck. The "Intsik" Pawa was about to kill the Supremo but was prevented from doing so. Was it personal hatred for Andres Bonifacio or did the contingent have orders to get him dead or alive?

Gregoria de Jesus, Bonifacio's widow, in a letter to Jacinto, later expressed her belief that the plan was to provoke her husband, and if he reacted, to kill him. (She also mentioned Colonel Intong's attempt to rape her. It will never be known whether it was just an attempt, for her entire testimony at the trial was either excised or lost.)

The Aguinaldo officers had a different version in the records of investigation conducted by Magdalo officers. Testimonies were taken down from 29 April to 4 May, when Andres Bonifacio and Gregoria de Jesus testified. The investigators found a prima facie case, and such was the efficiency of the Revolutionary Government that the court-martial was convened on the same day under the chairmanship of General Mariano Noriel. The trial was over in two days. The verdict: death to the Bonifacio brothers.

The decision of the Council of War, as the court-martial was called, came to President Aguinaldo on 7 May. In his own words:

> ... *when the* Expediente *came into my hands, I decided to commute the sentence to exile.*
>
> *As soon as General Mariano Noriel, General Pio del Pilar ... learned of this (commutation), they called my attention and said, 'If you want to maintain the stability of the Revolutionary Government and if you wish that we should stay alive, please withdraw your edict for those brothers.' Because of this, I withdrew and assigned General Noriel to follow the verdict of the Council of War, to shoot the brothers for the good of the country.*

This statement was written and signed in Aguinaldo's own hand, dated 22 March 1948, from Kawit, Cavite.

In a book entitled, *A Second Look at America*, written in collaboration with Vicente Albano Pacis (Robert Speller & Sons, Publishers, Inc. 1950), Aguinaldo was more descriptive about the Supremo.

> *The contrast between Bonifacio's defeats and my victories inevitably led to a general demand among our men for a drastic reorganization of our political and military leadership.*

And further on, referring to the Tejeros convention:

> *It was probably natural that Bonifacio should have been keenly disappointed and resentful over the election's result. As the* Katipunan's *founder, he perhaps had the right to believe that he should have been maintained*

as the head of the Revolution regardless of the fortunes or misfortunes of the cause. I could well understand the grief of his mind and the agony of his soul when, to stave off the complete collapse of our war for freedom, the convention ousted him as leader.

Relating his commutation order, he said

he had to yield to Generals Mariano Noriel and Pio del Pilar because of such practical possibilities ranging from "my assassination (proved by direct testimony) to joining forces with the Spaniards."

He also called Bonifacio a "counter-revolutionist," a word most probably supplied by his collaborator.

The burden of the execution was now laid on General Noriel, who ... had considered my withdrawal of my commutation order as confirmation of the Court Martial's decision. It had been my intention to delay my own final decision on Bonifacio until my subordinates had cooled off. During and immediately after the trial, they had been openly hostile to him.... Not only because of their resentment of his defiance of our authority but perhaps also out of loyalty to me.

Noriel offered another reason for his decision:

The Spaniards were about to attack and he feared the possibility of their liberating Bonifacio and his men or taking them as captives (!).

As stated before, Aguinaldo told a Spanish correspondent that the Supremo was a cruel man whom he ordered shot. But how the Supremo's revolutionary life came to such a pass was explained by his loyal ally, Santiago V. Alvarez in a rather strange way:

In the tempest that broke out at the Tejeros Assembly, the Supremo Bonifacio did not at once take precautions to guide his craft in such a way as to shield it from the storm; when he realized that he was losing grip, he was already far adrift. Only then did he try to steer his craft to a sheltered place. But, alas, he chose the village of Limbon (in Indang, Cavite) where the rocks against which his boat could be smashed were bigger...

History tells us of the sad and bitter end of the Supremo Bonifacio's odyssey in Cavite. Justice was not served and the sacrifices of life and blood, not only by the Supremo himself but also by other patriotic brethren, were they in vain? (Malay translation from the original Tagalog.)

The Supremo was either too politically naïve or insensitive to the situation, sensing too late his isolation. Not deceived?

But consider what his predicament was in Cavite. With every dark intention, the Magdalo faction did not recognize his leadership; in any case, it was thought best or expedient to eliminate it systematically from Imus to Tejeros. On the other hand, the Magdiwang used his authority as Supremo to overcome Aguinaldo's ascendancy. Santiago V. Alvarez was full of praises for him in his memoirs, but he would fault the Supremo for lack of prudence in staying too long in hostile territory. He did not "see" that his "boat was sinking" in the midst of the rivalry between the Magdiwang and Magdalo, a rivalry that often threatened to break out into open warfare but was always prevented *by the bravery and selflessness of their leaders*. However, no one could prevent the injustice done to their Supremo.

The crisis of the hero was not of his own making. In the first place, he was literally importuned and begged into coming to Cavite when he could just as easily have stayed in Balara or gone to Bulacan or Nueva Ecija.

But chroniclers and commentators would refer to his lack of political skills, his lack of knowledge that revolutions had to undergo contests of leadership, more exactly, struggles for power. That may very well be so, but the hero's tragic fate in Cavite was not, strictly, of his own making.

The hero's crisis did not originate in Tejeros; it simply unraveled there. If the Supremo had any personal responsibility for his crisis, it was for his decision to come to Cavite.

Lakanbini

Lakanbini *is the beautiful* nom de guerre *given to Gregoria de Jesus when she married Andres Bonifacio and became a member of the* Katipunan. *Today, the word means 'muse', but in the* Katipunan *context it probably meant First Woman, for although there was a woman's auxiliary in the early days of the* Katipunan, *Gregoria de Jesus was the first woman full-fledged member. Later on,* Lakanbini *could mean 'First Lady' when her husband became Supremo on 31 December 1895.*

"Oriang," as Gregoria was fondly called, was eighteen years old when she married Andres Bonifacio first in a church wedding, in deference to her parents' religious sensibilities, and then in Katipunan rites, in obedience to the revolutionary code. It was a courtship that took a year and a half to bear fruit. The year was taken up by Andres' earnest suit with Oriang's parents, who actually rejected him for being a freemason and therefore an evil man. Oriang's parents, like most parents then and now, were very much taken in by the propaganda of the *frailocracy.*

Nicolas de Jesus was a man of some substance in his native Caloocan, being a *gobernadorcillo* or town mayor; he was a master mason and carpenter. His wife was Baltazara Alvarez Francisco from Noveleta, a niece of Katipunan General Mariano Alvarez, father of Santiago V. Alvarez. Oriang obviously inherited her "rebellious" nature from her mother's line. Her parents could do nothing but consent to her marriage when Oriang made it very clear that she was very much in love with the thirty-year old widower, freemason, and founder of the secret revolutionary society called the Katipunan.

The first tragedy of her life was the loss of an infant son named after her father, doubtless the consequence of her arduous life as a Katipunera. To her were entrusted the important documents of the Society, which she wrapped around her body beneath her dress whenever she set forth on the Revolution's business. Her house was often filled from dusk to dawn with men administering and taking the oath of the Society.

"Many times on receiving some warning that the house would be searched by the *Veterana* police, regardless of the hour, I would immediately gather all the papers, the arms and the seal, and order a *quiles* (a horse-drawn carriage with closed windows), abandoning my meals for quite often this happened at noon or eight o'clock at night," she recalled in her *Tala* of 5 November 1928.

"I would go on driving until midnight along the bay front of Tondo and the streets of Binondo in order to save our countrymen from danger. The thing that grieved me, however, was the fact that whenever I asked some friends, whom I expected to be cooperative, for help, they would refuse and even keep away from me, upon knowing that I was carrying dangerous things."

When the Revolution broke out, she learned to ride and shoot. Considered a soldier in her own right, she witnessed and participated in not a few encounters with the enemy. Her extraordinary courage and alertness—she was never captured by the enemy—was spoken of by Katipunan generals. She knew what it was to sleep hungry and cold on the ground, to drink dirty water from mud-holes or "the sap of vines, which though bitter, tasted delicious because of my intense thirst. When I came to think of my life in those days, considering my youth then, I am surprised how I stood it all, and how I was spared."

But in the end this was to prove of little discomfort compared to her second tragedy: the loss of her husband. In Limbon, Indang, she witnessed the death of the Supremo's brother Ciriaco, the wounding of the Supremo himself, and the arrest of all their companions. Oriang, by her account before the Council of War, narrowly escaped from the lustful designs of Agapito Bonzon, alias Colonel Intong. But as the full transcript of her testimony was either lost or excised from the documents of the trial, one could only guess at the seriousness of Intong's offense. There is no record that he was made to account for it.

After the infamous trial, she never saw the Supremo again, although she tried every avenue of appeal and supplication.

Asked to recall those days—the "controversy between Bonifacio and Aguinaldo which culminated in the execution of Bonifacio," she would say nothing more than refer to her letter to Emilio Jacinto, "which according to General Cipriano Pacheco, is now in the hands of Jose P. Santos."

It was obvious she did not want to relive the event after having related it once to a dear friend and comrade. Thereafter, the family of her second husband, the valiant Julio Nakpil, shielded her from the curiosity of historians and writers.

The rest of her life was summed up by her translator, the scholar Dr. Encarnacion Alzona:

When the Revolution was suppressed by the Americans, Gregoria de Jesus returned to peaceful life. Now married to another patriot, Julio Nakpil, she became a devoted wife and mother, but still loyal to the ideals of the Revolution which she instilled in the minds of her children. Following the precept of the Katipunan, *she educated all her children to be industrious and useful to their country. She saw to it that she cultivated their individual talents and led purposeful lives. She was not disappointed for she lived long enough to see them esteemed by the public for their artistic and professional achievements.*

Gregoria de Jesus vda. de Bonifacio y Nakpil, born on 9 May 1875, died 15 March 1943, in the dark days of the Japanese Occupation at the age of 68.

Aside from the tumultuous life she led with the tragic hero of the Revolution, she also left a testament of her love for him in two poems, one written 31 August 1897 and the other on September of the same year, composed more than three and four months after his disappearance from her life.

Death will bring us
Together again.

CHAPTER FIVE

Death of the Hero

N
o historian or chronicler of the Revolution has claimed that Andres Bonifacio had a fair trial. That it was a mockery of justice was officially passed over in silence until Supreme Court Justice Abraham F. Sarmiento, in a tour de force exercise of judicial judgment, acquitted the Accused in a learned paper commemorating the 129th birth anniversary of the Hero in 1992. He called the execution of Andres and Procopio Bonifacio our history's "greatest unsolved mystery."

The mystery, of course, is not the trial and death itself but the reason(s) behind it, as it was clear from Day One that Andres Bonifacio and his brother Procopio were going to be found guilty and given the death sentence. One follows from the other: if Bonifacio was guilty of plotting the assassination of the President of the Revolutionary government, then he deserved the death penalty, and since it was clear that he would be found guilty, then it followed that he would die.

The last hundred years have not resolved the controversy over the execution of Andres Bonifacio. Epifanio de los Santos reduces the matter into a "kill or be killed" situation in which Bonifacio is seen as a threat to the Revolution. He accepted Bonifacio's natural intolerance, saying that it was the effect of his hard life both as a working man and a revolutionist.

Bonifacio's existence (wrote Epifanio de los Santos), was:

...one of constant struggle in every instant of his busy life, surrounded by obstacles which any person but he would have found impossible to overcome. While earning his daily bread by modest and despised occupation, he had to

combat his own ignorance and educate himself, and to found, educate, and instruct at the same time the puritanical society that was his work, defend himself and defend it against a regime that had all corrupting and stifling influences at its disposal, and finally, without any means of his own, defeat the enemy with his own arms, not in a battle fought at random, but in hundreds of battles in which the probabilities of being annihilated forever amounted to at least 99 percent.

He therefore lacked that tact and self-control which can only be acquired in a propitiate, favorable atmosphere. (Some would describe tact and self-control, in our context, as the Machiavellian capacity for mendacity.)

This recalls another historian's pronouncement on the ambitious urban poor as a politically volatile class, as if only the better off and educated were capable of selfless patriotism.

But de los Santos withdraws, tempering his judgment with the observation that Bonifacio "was capable of veneration, admiration, and sacrifice," for his seemingly cruel and impious qualities were "but the bitter rind of a fruit the meat of which was luscious and delicious, because at the bottom he was religious, a true believer, and possessed of the best sentiments and national aptitudes." The good chronicler was wrong: the Katipunan, not without Bonifacio's consent, required its own marriage ritual for Andres and Gregoria de Jesus in spite of their church wedding. The "Sons of the People" did not recognize a marriage officiated by a priest as legitimate. And if Bonifacio was a true believer, it was not in the conventional religious sense: his faith lay in the "Sons of the People."

This ambivalent attitude towards Andres Bonifacio persists to this day among many scholars and historians. It is as if they cannot wholly extend to a plebeian hero the same reverence that they have for the ilustrado hero and martyr. In reconciling the hero with the tragedy, they cannot do better than Epifanio de los Santos, who in repeating but giving no credence to the whisperings against Bonifacio in Cavite, concludes that "not only the leaders of Cavite and other provinces contributed to the death of Andres Bonifacio, but also the unconscious mass of the people which, in a situation as critical as that, could not be expected to show serenity of judgment and prudence." In a word, Andres Bonifacio was done in by intrigues. But who fomented the intrigues and why?

In a passionate appeal for understanding and national unity, De los Santos declares:

> *The most charitable and humane is therefore to attribute things to error, grave error, if you will, on the part of all and nobody, and all are, therefore, entitled to filial pardon, seeing that their errors would, after all, have been our own had we been placed in their position, though our "amour propre" might wish to disown them and our hypocrisy be anxious to conceal them.*

How elegant and moving must this passage be in the original Spanish! It is once noble and conciliatory, forgiving of all who fought in the Revolution, recognizing all sacrifices, with Bonifacio's life as the greatest sacrifice of all. He founded the Katipunan which made the Revolution. His execution was a grave error.

Well and good. That should put the matter to rest.

The trouble, however, is the relentless research into our past. A new breed of historians like Milagros C. Guerrero have unearthed some documents which will reopen rather than close old wounds. In an article entitled "Aguinaldo's Secret," Guerrero cited a number of Filipino and Spanish sources detailing Emilio Aguinaldo's attempts to negotiate for peace with the Spaniards as early as March 1897, days before the fateful Tejeros convention. The intermediaries, were a Jesuit priest, Pio Pi and a journalist, Rafael Comenge, whose overtures Aguinaldo found *laudable y provechoso* (laudable and profitable). Guerrero finds a significant relation between this and Bonifacio's letter to Emilio Jacinto dated 24 April 1897 in which the former alludes to Aguinaldo's *deslealtad* (disloyalty), arising from his desire to surrender the Revolution. But the negotiator for Spain withdrew, fearing the Aguinaldo might demand concessions that his superiors were not prepared to consider. Further, a telegraphic correspondence between General Manuel Galbis in Guadalupe, Makati and Governor Camilo Polavieja in January 1897—much earlier than the proposed negotiations in March—reveals that Aguinaldo had sought a "conference" with the Spaniards through the cura of Pateros. Polavieja referred to Aguinaldo's initiative in a letter to Manuel Azcarraga, minister of the colonies, on 4 February 1897: *"Ya, Emilio Aguinaldo, por medio de un fraile, ha intentado venir a tratos, pretendienda pactos concesiones politicos."* In plain words, Aguinaldo, through a friar, seeks an agreement on political concessions. Polavieja then instructed General Galbis to tell Aguinaldo that he should take advantage of the proffered pardon or else the government would pursue the rebellion and its leaders *"con gran energia."* By February, Polavieja could be firm as the Spaniards had "repossessed" Silang, Dasmariñas, Salitran, and Imus.

Guerrero concludes from these documents that Andres Bonifacio's death had become imperative. Emilio Aguinaldo ordered Bonifacio's arrest on 27 April 1897. This came two months *after* Aguinaldo had sought to negotiate with Polavieja and a month *after* he had been elected president of the revolutionary government in Tejeros.

From this angle, the Tejeros Assembly, called to unify the rival Magdiwang and Magdalo factions and to decide the course of the war, was actually planned to behead the Katipunan as the government of the Revolution. It was rigged against the Katipunan and Bonifacio, so that a revolutionary government, headed by Aguinaldo, could take the direction of the revolution, including compromise with the Spanish authorities.

But it was not until eight months later, 14 December 1897, that the truce of Biak-na-Bato was signed through the intercession of Pedro Paterno, who was said to be aspiring for a dukedom. (He did not get it.) The terms were the surrender of rebel arms, the exile of Aguinaldo and other leaders to Hong Kong, the sum of P400,000 paid to Aguinaldo, the first P200,000 upon the surrender of 1,500 guns, and the balance when the terms had been complied with. It must be noted too that part of the reason the truce pushed through was that Madrid, two months before, had instructed Governor-General Primo de Rivera to negotiate "with the utmost secrecy" and "greatest possible haste."

The process took some time but the fact remains that Aguinaldo was thinking of negotiation and "compromise" in early March—before the fateful Tejeros convention. If this is the motive, or one of the motives, for the trial and execution of Bonifacio, the solution to the mystery is certainly disturbing.

Aguinaldo apparently incriminated himself in an interview with the reporter of *El Imparcial* as he prepared to leave for Hong Kong in 1898:

> *We took the field not because we wished for separation from the mother country, which gave us her laws, her religion, her customs, her language, and her way of thinking, but because we were tired of bearing the material and moral burden laid on us by that arch, the keystone of which in our country is the friars. It is quite true that the* Katipunan *instilled in us another desire—that of independence—but that desire was unattainable, and moreover it was in opposition to our sentiments. It served as the banner of Andres Bonifacio, a cruel man whom I ordered shot and with his death the* Katipunan *disappeared. You may be sure of this: we ask no reforms other than that the influence the friars hold under the laws in all our towns be restrained. We do not ask for their expulsion, for such radical measures should not be carried into effect under present conditions. We desire that the parishes be secularized or that they be presided over by friars who depend, not on their provincials, but on the archbishop, and, in a measure, we ask that some part of the patrimony of the* haciendas *in the provinces be diverted from the religious orders to us.*

This was reformist talk and a grave indictment of Bonifacio before the world. True, Aguinaldo could just be lulling the Spaniards into a false sense of security as he embarked for Hong Kong to buy arms for another try at revolution. But the statement about ordering Bonifacio's execution is quite revealing, since in his memoirs, he also accused Bonifacio of wanting to destroy the revolution. Recalling the capture of Imus by General Zabala on 28 February 1897, a defeat that he blamed on Bonifacio's supposed orders to Gen. Artemio Ricarte to intercept the Magdalo forces, Aguinaldo wrote:

> *When I realized what the* Supremo *had done I sighed and said to myself, "He wished to destroy our Revolution." General Mariano Trias, in*

anger, recommended that the traitors be arrested. What did our country, aspiring for freedom, gain from that loathsome act and selfish purpose?

He did not say why Bonifacio and Ricarte were not arrested. Or was he just waiting for the proper time, at least in Bonifacio's case, since Artemio Ricarte, despite Bonifacio's execution, or because of it, served Aguinaldo's revolutionary government?

At the very least, the statement to the Spanish paper and the memoirs, reveal a hostility towards Bonifacio even before the Tejeros Assembly.

Before Spain and the world and Revolution, Emilio Aguinaldo accused Bonifacio of perfidy. To Spain and the world, Bonifacio virtually imposed revolution on the Katipuneros, at least on Aguinaldo and his followers, and before the people, he wanted to destroy "our" Revolution. The hero, in the language of our time, was surrounded on all planks.

An independent investigation into the circumstances that led to the Supremo's "liquidation" could create, on the basis of these passages and other evidence, a conspiracy theory. The key would be Daniel Tirona's unbelievable behavior towards the Supremo when he arrived in Cavite on December 1896, upon the invitation of the Magdiwang faction. Accompanied by twenty men, Gregoria de Jesus, and his two brothers, Bonifacio was "warmly received along the way" by the Caviteños, among them Daniel Tirona, shouting in the streets, "Long live the Supreme President of the Katipunan," "Long live the King of the Philippines," to which Bonifacio reacted, "Long live the liberty of the Philippines."

But some weeks later, the same Tirona circulated leaflets attacking Bonifacio as a freemason and atheist (Aguinaldo was himself a freemason), violating everything holy, trampling on the crucifix, a man of little education and a German spy. Confronted by his victim, Tirona refused to give a satisfactory answer, forcing the former to draw out his revolver. Only the intervention of the women saved Tirona, as another intervention by Ricarte would again spare his life four months later in the Tejeros Assembly.

There is no explanation for Tirona's behavior, considering that Bonifacio trusted him well enough to include him in the delegation that negotiated for arms with the Japanese Admiral Hirawa. What was his purpose? Clearly, to discredit Bonifacio before the Caviteños, but to what end? This appears to be explained by his attempt to block Bonifacio's election as Minister of Interior, which finally provoked the hero into the fatal step of nullifying the proceedings and forming, in Zaide's words, "his own government." By that act, he became an illegal in the eyes of the newly constituted Aguinaldo government.

Still, that there was a conspiracy must be proven beyond the shadow of a doubt. The evidence for it is circumstantial. But only the most naïve can say in confidence that the Tejeros Assembly was above board in every respect. Tirona was allowed to make his disruptive speech. Was he alone in his purpose, or was he part of a wider design? That is the "unsolved mystery."

But we are by no means through. There is also the mystery of the circumstances of his death. According to an eyewitness account, Andres Bonifacio did not die a hero's death. He was not as calm as Jose Rizal, nor was he as defiant as General Antonio Luna who shouted at his assassins, "Cowards!" Instead, he grabbed his executioner's legs, begged for his life, and when he realized that it was futile, made a desperate dash for the woods of Mt. Buntis, where he was overtaken and shot to death.

This was the account of Major Lazaro Macapagal, Bonifacio's executioner, in his handwritten letter in Tagalog to Jose P. Santos, 27 June 1929. (There was, in fact, another "recollection" by the same Macapagal.) He was accompanied by four soldiers but only he had made a written account thirty-two years after the event.

Macapagal began by saying that he had not promptly responded to Santos's request for an account because the incident had occurred long ago, that probably "all around" already knew it.

He related that on the morning of 10 May 1897, at the time the Spanish forces attacked Maragondon, General Noriel told him: "Commandant, this packet is for you but you are not to open it, and here's what you must do. Make haste to the prison and request Colonel Ritual for four soldiers to accompany you to Ermita where you will fetch the brothers Andres and Procopio Bonifacio. Take them to Mount

Tala and, upon arrival, open this packet and read aloud its contents to the two of them and you obey them strictly, this must be done with dispatch because the Spaniards are (at the gates)."

Macapagal went forth to carry out his verbal orders. On their way to Tala, the brothers asked him whether they were going to be shot, but he said he was just taking them away from the fighting. He added that all he knew was orders and work.

As they reached Maragondon, the brothers asked for a respite (Bonifacio, after all, was wounded in the neck and shoulders). They were now in Mount Buntis, and the Bonifacio brothers asked him to read what was in the sealed packet, since they were already near their destination.

> Commandant L. Macapagal (the executioner read aloud), according to the orders of the Council of War held at Maragondon on the eighth of May against the brothers G. Andres and Procopio Bonifacio, (they) were sentenced to be shot to death.
>
> You (Macapagal) and the soldiers under your authority have been assigned to accomplish the said task of shooting the two brothers.
>
> I am informing you that any failure to do your duty will be penalized to the fullest severity of the Spanish military law.
>
> God will take care of you for a long time.

The order was signed Mariano Noriel.

The brothers were stunned. Macapagal reached for his revolver because Procopio, unlike Andres, was unhurt. He was the first to be shot as he ran to the woods, after which, Macapagal returned to Bonifacio. He had to do his duty with a heavy heart, for if he had known what the packet contained, he would not have accepted it. Back in Maragondon, he was accosted by Gregoria de Jesus, who inquired about her now slain husband, and all he could say was to ask the President in Tala. Wounded by the Spanish bombardment, he would have welcomed death than carry in his heart the burden of his deed. But he had no alternative; he was a soldier of the Revolution. Besides, it would have meant his own death.

What grabs the throat in Macapagal's account was not only his great remorse but the "cowardice" of Andres Bonifacio and his brother. The hero, so valorous in battle, could not face with courage the prospect of his own death.

This is not easy to accept, and yet there is no other account but that of Major Lazaro Macapagal's. Would he have had any motive for embellishing or economizing on the truth? If this was his original story to his superiors, he had to be consistent with it thirty-two years later. President Emilio Aguinaldo and some of his generals were still alive then.

It would certainly be amiss to portray Andres Bonifacio as heroic in death. Andres Bonifacio was denied a hero's death, for a hero must die in battle against the avowed enemy. It was an inglorious death, but it had to be inglorious for him and not for the people who ordered his death. Making him out as a coward would somehow justify the deed.

Bonifacio, it must be said, had an image of himself as the bravest of men. This he had proved in organizing the Katipunan and calling for revolution even before the August week of 1896. Would he have "revealed" his "cowardly streak" just as he realized that everything was lost? It goes against all human psychology for a consistently brave and even irascible man, who would face a duel at any personal affront (and in the face of so many, who could be his enemies) to suddenly break down at the prospect of death, whatever the identity of his assassin.

Nevertheless, the lover and advocate of Andres Bonifacio must confront the damaging testimony of Major Lazaro Macapagal. He can choose not to believe all its details but one: that Macapagal shot the Bonifacio brothers to death. He did not bury them properly, "as a matter of respect (emphasized he)," but there was no shovel around. They just dug a bit with their bayonets and covered the body with wood branches. Macapagal and his companions hurried out of the scene.

In confronting Macapagal's account, we should recall that he was the secretary of the Council of War that tried and condemned the Supremo. And he said that he did not know what was in store for the Bonifacio brothers!

He also said that he walked Bonifacio to Mount Tala, a man whose wounds on the neck and shoulders were unattended for eleven days (or were the medical records lost?), and most probably suffering from gangrene. This gives credence to a contrary account that a farmer had witnessed the execution. A man on a hammock was hacked to death by five men.

The hero, deprived in life, was deprived in death. And so did the Revolution "devour" its father.

That is the tragedy of the Philippine Revolution.

CHAPTER SIX

The Tragedy of the Revolution

Historians called the death of Andres Bonifacio *a* tragedy of the Revolution. Some of them are content to call it the tragedy of Andres Bonifacio. But there is more reason to recognize it as *the* Tragedy *of* the Revolution.

Epifanio de los Santos y Cristobal, caught in his tandem admiration for Bonifacio and Aguinaldo, offered the view that unjust as the trial and execution of Andres Bonifacio was, it was humane and charitable to regard it as a "grave error." The two Kalaws, Dean Maximo and Teodoro (like de los Santos, a scholar and former director of the National Library) pronounced it "necessary."

"The revolutionists could not afford to be divided," said Dean Kalaw. "One or two courses had to be taken: either the continuation of the Katipunan Government under Bonifacio or the maintenance of the new Revolutionary Government under Aguinaldo which had the support of the majority...The Revolutionary Government was forced to eliminate him."

The other Kalaw said "...the facts, judged *a posteriori*, sustained Aguinaldo's point of view. Unity had to be maintained....All opposition had to be put down with an iron hand."

This view was probably acceptable in the days when "revolutionary necessity" was yet to be employed in the purges and genocide of the twentieth century. But even during the French Revolution, "the high principles of the Revolution" clothed every act of the codified murders of the simply inconvenient and disagreeable. "Revolutionary necessity" then and now is a thin excuse for the execution of the *father* of the Revolution.

Revolutions devour their children but the *fathers*—Lenin, Mao Ze Dong, Ho Chi Minh, Fidel Castro (whatever our feeling ideological or otherwise, about them) were more devouring than devoured. Perhaps, it was because they, unlike Andres Bonifacio, were stronger than the children of the revolution.

In his memoirs, Emilio Aguinaldo reduced the matter into a "kill-or-be-killed" proposition. Fifty-three years later, Aguinaldo called Bonifacio a "counter-revolutionist," in *A Second Look At America*.

But a counter-revolution is precisely a reversal of the revolution, a surrender, in this instance, to Spain, the prevailing power—something that Bonifacio was not about to do. Instead, in his letter to Jacinto, Bonifacio accused Aguinaldo of trying to negotiate a truce with the Spaniards. (This was finally accomplished in the Pact of Biak-na-Bato on 14 December 1897.)

If at all, it was Aguinaldo who could be more credibly accused of counter-revolution if Bonifacio had lived to extract his revenge, as his former lieutenant, Pio del Pilar, had intimated to Aguinaldo. This would sustain the cynical wisdom that history is written by the victors.

Historian Teodoro A. Agoncillo and scholar Silvino V. Epistola objected to the view of Aguinaldo as a counter-revolutionist. They attributed the Tragedy of the Revolution to a conflict of leadership, not of ideology, a result of factional rivalry between Magdiwang and Magdalo, compounded by age-old regionalism between *verdadero Manileño* and *verdadero Caviteño*—and the contempt of a very small group of educated men like Clemente Jose Zulueta, Mamerto Natividad, Feliciano Jocson, and Edilberto Evangelista (he of the rejected constitution), for the lowly Supremo. Non-Caviteños, they nevertheless voted against Bonifacio who had accused them of "dickering" with the Jesuit agents Pio Pi and Rafael Comenge.

"Bonifacio, then, was confronted with two hostile forces: regionalism, on the one hand, and the elite group, on the other. His failure to get elected to the highest position dramatized the role played by those forces."

With this all-embracing explanation, Agoncillo and Epistola attributed Bonifacio's fall to his disappointment—resentment, if you will—at not being elected president of the Revolutionary Government.

But the record shows that he only lost his temper after Daniel Tirona had questioned his election as Secretary of Interior. Would he have walked out all the same if his election as Secretary of Interior had proceeded smoothly?

In refusing to confront the tragedy of the Revolution, several writers cling to the compromise of blaming regionalism, elitism, and leadership conflicts, for the arrest, trial, and execution of Andres Bonifacio. The implication is that forces, or circumstances, beyond the control of Andres Bonifacio and Emilio Aguinaldo presided like the Greek Furies over the fate of the hero.

From the accounts of Bonifacio's character and the behavior of his detractors, it is easy to construct a drama along the lines of Shakespeare's *Tragedy of Julius Caesar*. In the play, Caesar was thrice offered the crown and rejected it, as was hailed more than once as "Supremo," even "King," to which he invariably replied, "Long Live the Motherland," emphasizing his submission to the revolutionary cause. Meanwhile, as the Roman populace was acclaiming Caesar, a scheming Cassius was working on Brutus to regard Caesar as a danger to the Republic—as his cohorts did to Aguinaldo. Caesar did not heed the warning about the "Ides of March," and Bonifacio, the omens in Cavite. Caesar went to the Senate without any idea of what was in store for him, Bonifacio went to Tejeros without any idea of the plot against him and the Katipunan.

The difference was that Caesar, realizing the treachery of his "son" Brutus (*Et tu, Brute?*), embraced the dagger, while Bonifacio, realizing the treachery of those whom he thought were "Sons of the People," left in a rage.

Standing over Caesar's corpse, Brutus accused the assassinated of overweening ambition. In life, death, and after death, Bonifacio was accused of the same offense. The posthumous judgment on Andres Bonifacio centered on his supposed presumption that as the Supremo of the Katipunan, he ought to have been the president of the Tejeros-installed Revolutionary Government. This was his "tragic flaw," the *hubris*, characteristic of the heroes of Shakespearean and Greek tragedies.

Above all, Bonifacio was also "hot-tempered and thus created many enemies, who, however, survived him. He had no military successes"—

a debatable proposition to brag about principally because Bonifacio preferred guerrilla warfare; although by threatening Manila, he threw the center of colonial power into a panic, which, in turn, encouraged other provinces to join the Revolution. "He was of humble origins, had precious little education and so was unfit for the leadership he considered as rightfully his."

As Agoncillo and Epistola pointed out, "it was not until the second phase of the Revolution, when Bonifacio had unwillingly left the stage, that sophisticated men appeared on the scene."

Combining the concepts of Shakespearean and Greek tragedies, Andres Bonifacio was ambitious, on the one hand, and born under a tragic star, on the other. He accomplished the heroic deed of organizing the revolutionary Katipunan among people plagued by regionalism, factionalism, and elitism, proudly thinking, in his hubris, that he was the voice, the conscience, the heart and soul of the Revolution.

But while the literary tragedies gave us catharsis, a purging of the emotions out of the experience of pity and horror, the real tragedy of Andres Bonifacio excites strong feelings of rage and shame. The reason is that one hundred years after his death, Andres Bonifacio is still being tried by specious means by scholars with dubious motives.

The most recent attack, timed for the centenary of Bonifacio's execution, came from an American historian, who, after questioning the veracity of Filipino writers, memoirists and historians—Ricarte, de los Santos, Agoncillo, etc.—arrived at the astonishing conclusion that Andres Bonifacio was a "flawed hero." Not one with a tragic flaw, but simply flawed. All heroes are "flawed" in one way or another, but only in the sense that they are human, but what the American wanted to convey was that Bonifacio's "flaws" (which he did not document, much less discuss) did not entitle him to be called a hero. Many Filipino historians have refuted in force the malicious assertions. Nevertheless, it is tragic that this has to be done, for there are also other Filipino historians who tend to endow sheer malice with respectability.

Exasperating as this recent attack on Bonifacio may be, it is lamentably injurious and insulting to hear otherwise learned Filipino scholars maintain that Bonifacio's life and death was merely part of a "historical process." This gives a scholarly scent to the fallacy that what happened to him was justified for the very reason that it happened. History is the infallible god to which mere mortals could only submit.

But if the moral and legal reasons given for the arrest, trial, and execution of Andres Bonifacio fail to convince (in spite of the widely circulated versions of his executioners), then a crime was committed against the Supremo of the Katipunan. And if it was a crime, its perpetrators must be judged as criminals, even if it is too late to bring them to justice in the usual sense.

The problem, however, is that it was the perpetrators who accused and condemned Andres Bonifacio as a criminal, even as latter day historians recognized his place in the heroic history of the race. This is an embarrassment, to say the least, since both the innocent as well as the guilty (whether it be Bonifacio, Aguinaldo, or assorted executioners) have been given their places in the pantheon of Filipino heroes.

It is no solution to a national shame to say that all were heroes but that they had their own faults. No crime can be so easily dismissed.

Either Andres Bonifacio was guilty or he was not. The answer, "Both—from a relative point of view," is a moral and intellectual swindle. That cannot be a comfort for historians whose vocation is to find out the truth about what happened. More than that, it is no balm to a people still smarting from the wounds of a hundred years. It is a shabby legacy not only for our generation but future generations as well.

I delivered a lecture on 10 May 1997 in memory of the centenary of Bonifacio's execution. A day later, I was told by two friends that a young man from Cavite had arrived after the end of the open forum. He introduced himself as a descendant of Emilio Aguinaldo, adding that his purpose in coming to the lecture was to convey the apologies of the Aguinaldo family for what had been done to Andres Bonifacio. No one, however, got his name, and I am not sure that he truly was an Aguinaldo, or if he was, if he had any authority to speak for the family. He could also have been a hoax.

Still, I wish he could have come on time for the open forum. It would have been the most sensational news of our Centennial.

The gesture, even if it were not authorized by the family, would have been significant if he were an authentic Aguinaldo descendant. The historical cloud that three generations could not lift might have been lifted by a fourth removed by time from passion and partisanship.

The truth is that the controversy over the life and death of Andres Bonifacio is inflamed by partisanship. Descendants of Aguinaldo and Bonifacio, not to mention the Magdiwang and Magdalo, abound. Aguinaldo's descendants occupy prominent places in society while those of Bonifacio are, not surprisingly, "common people."

Writers and intellectuals are also divided between what a wag calls "Bonifascists" and "Aguinaldolts," a facetious remark reflective of uneasiness. Nevertheless, it is interesting to note that Andres Bonifacio's allies had more telling things to say about his executioners than what the executioners had to say of him. Among these were Julio Nakpil, the second husband of Gregoria de Jesus, the hero's widow; Masangkay, Alvarez, and Mabini.

In his notes on Kalaw's *The Philippine Revolution*, Nakpil, with unconcealed hatred of Aguinaldo, tells of the Revolutionary Government's attempts to purge the leading members of the Katipunan. He also related an incident in which as Minister of Development (*Fomento*) of the Revolutionary Government, he suggested the continuation of the Katipunan "for the purpose of collecting more funds for the acquisition of firearms, telling them that the Katipunan revolutionists and even outsiders had very great faith in the Katipunan. Mr. Emilio Aguinaldo took this ill and without any further explanation ordered General Severino Taiño and Pio del Pilar to assassinate me. Is it perchance fair to kill a person, even supposing him to be delinquent, without having heard his testimony and without due process of law? The fact is that I have not received any reply and naturally I was of the belief that they approved my idea."

It appears that *they* did. In mid-July 1898, on the second phase of the Philippine Revolution, Aguinaldo appealed to the Katipuneros to rejoin the Katipunan. According to the excerpt extracted by O. D. Corpuz, Aguinaldo recognized them as the "men who opened up the road, the first to expose themselves to the dangers in front of us to liberate and save the people from the claws of cruelty and baseness." No one could deny the Katipuneros the fame and honor they gained by their glorious acts.

> *Nevertheless, think: formerly the members of the* Katipunan *were marked with a sign in order that the true brothers might know each other; that is not the case now because the day so hoped for by us has now arrived when all born in the Filipinas recognize each other as true brothers; there is no* Katipunan *today because the entire Filipinas, our dear most mother country, is the true* Katipunan *in which all her sons are united and agreed in one desire and one wish, that is, to rescue the mother country which groans in slavery.*

The Katipuneros poignantly answered that they were the virtual poor cousins of the "Revolutionary Army," so "always trusting in the uprightness and magnanimity of Aguinaldo," they would rather be mustered out in order to attend to their families and their labors. They had not forgotten the purge that the Revolutionary Government carried out against the Katipuneros after Bonifacio's execution. (The Society of the Sons of the People was revived in late 1899 when Aguinaldo decided to wage war against the Americans, precisely the kind of war that the Katipuneros, outnumbered and without arms, began in Manila on August 1896.)

Alvarez recalled hearing that he was going to be arrested and tried two days after the capture of the Supremo, and he immediately rode to the house where Aguinaldo and his generals were staying. It was a tense moment, but Aguinaldo expressed the hope that he, Apoy, would not separate from them. He thought the same thing that Nakpil would later say: that the indignation of the relatives of the "murdered" suppressed their rage for the sake of unity.

The "turnaround" was condemned by Epifanio de los Santos in grandiloquent terms:

> *After the* Katipunan *had become a success, there came an influx of false* Katipuneros, *whose excesses brought discredit upon the society. Men like beasts, but who act like* mangy curs *when in misfortune, who are the first to pass over to the enemy with exaggerated protests of loyalty to the new*

*masters, after betraying the old, stabbing him in the back, and heaping
infamy, believing that by such villainies they prove their loyalty to the new
master and obtain his good will and favor.*

In a footnote, Agoncillo wrote his complete agreement on this point,
but as Nakpil pointed out, there were also those who did not shift loyalties
but simply remained true to the aims of the Revolution.

Many Katipuneros, however, were not so high-minded, if only
because their commitment to Revolution was also a deep personal
commitment to the Supremo.

Because of the death of the Supremo Bonifacio, many of the
dedicated patriots from Cavite, Manila, Rizal and Laguna, who were
defending the Revolution, lost heart and did not continue to serve the
Motherland; they neither participated nor got involved with any group
or any needs of the Revolution, they kept their distance, attending instead
to their wives and children and simply watched unfolding events. This
lack of enthusiasm further weakened the movement. In spite of the
satisfaction of some (over the elimination of the Supremo), there was a
sudden exodus from the towns occupied by the Revolution in Cavite;
many went back to their own business in fields and hills, and also returned
to their own provinces, (so wrote Santiago V. Alvarez).

Those who followed the Supremo feared reprisals on their own
person. It was like being hounded by the Civil Guards again. Perhaps, it
was paranoia, but what could simple Katipuneros living in what suddenly
had become a strange town think, seeing how their leader had been
executed by his own kind? The Katipunan tenet prohibited doing
violence to brothers, let alone killing them.

Mabini, a close adviser of Emilio Aguinaldo y Famy, the President
of the Revolutionary Government, was certain that "the tragic event
dampened the ardor for the cause of the Revolution and precipitated
the failure of the Revolution in Cavite, because many of those from
Manila, Laguna and Batangas who were fighting throughout the province
within withdrew, disgusted, and soon the so-called central government
had to be transferred to the mountains of Biak-na-Bato, from where it
never moved."

Epifanio de los Santos tried to refute Mabini's contention about the fading enthusiasm of the Katipuneros after Bonifacio's execution. However, this is contradicted by Aguinaldo's appeal to the Katipuneros in mid-July 1898, to which they replied with a delicious irony worthy of a Mabini.

"We are no longer Katipuneros."

At this juncture, we come to the spurious question of Andres Bonifacio's "generalship," narrowly defined as winning battles rather than directing them. In the *Notas* published (at his request) after his death, Julio Nakpil recalled how Andres Bonifacio had entreated him and Emilio Jacinto to launch a third attack on San Mateo *for the purpose of drawing away the attention of the Spanish forces toward other points and prevent their concentration on Kawit, Cavite.* Alvarez also tells of encounters in which the Magdalo were not as *beau geste* with their Magdiwang brothers.

Finally, was it really paranoia that made many Katipuneros distance themselves from the Revolutionary Government?

Apolinario Mabini's letter to Emilio Jacinto, then wounded in Laguna, dated 17 November 1898, from Malolos, Bulacan, spoke for itself:

My very dear Friend,

> *Many thanks for your present. During the first days, I pretended not to remember you, fearing that they would not approve of our friendship. I needed then all their faith in me so that I could give the stamp of regularity on the progress of the government, although I did not accomplish this fully.*
>
> *When I received your letter, I sent someone to ask Captain Emilio whether you could stay in Malolos with the assurance that nobody would bother you for what had taken place before. He answered yes, adding that you should forget everything ...*

Emilio Jacinto never had a chance to forgive and forget—Nakpil was definite he did not take the oath of allegiance to the Revolutionary

Government, for he died of his wound. On a romantic note, he had sent a piece of bone from his wounded thigh to Gregoria de Jesus.

Anyway, this guarded letter from the "brains of the Revolution" to the "brains of the Katipunan" says everything about the atmosphere in the aftermath of the hero's execution than any long, detailed description of the travails of the Katipuneros.

Finally, there was the irascible General Guillermo Masangkay, the hero's friend since their youthful days in Tondo. Some historians of the Revolution assert that Masangkay was not actually a general, as if being named a general in those days had to go through the Commission on Appointments. Valor was always quickly rewarded by promotion. Besides that, Masangkay was an original Katipunero.

In an interview given to journalist Luis Serrano in 31 May 1963, he reiterated an earlier vow never to have anything to do with Emilio Aguinaldo after his friend's execution. (He did not join the Veterans of the Philippine Revolution because it was headed by Aguinaldo.) Friendship may be cited as the root of Masangkay's prejudice, but then he was also the brother-in-law of General Noriel, the head of the Council of War that tried Bonifacio and Masangkay himself.

Reminded that it was the Council of War and not Aguinaldo which convicted the Brothers Bonifacio, Masangkay snorted, "That's what the history books say."

> The court martial? I ought to know about it. I was one of Bonifacio's men who had been arrested by Aguinaldo's men and indicted before the court. The court was headed by Noriel who was my brother-in-law. Noriel in later years disclosed the inner workings of the court in our more intimate moments. I learned that Aguinaldo had been behind every step taken by the court martial in the Bonifacio case. Aguinaldo appeared to have commuted the death sentence, but he rescinded the commutation and allowed the carrying out of the death sentence.

He also claimed that some of the men under Major Lazaro Macapagal told him how the hero was actually killed: not by bullets but by bolo and bayonet. "They decided that it would be a waste of bullets," said the doughty Katipunero.

Years later, he joined a group of government officials and scholars formed by Senate President Manuel Luis Quezon to search for the remains of the hero. It was headed by Secretary of the Interior Teofilo Sison, and its members were Secretary of Finance Elpidio Quirino; Representatives Benito Soliven and Fidel Villanueva; Professor Austin Craig, head of the history department of the University of the Philippines; Teodoro M. Kalaw, director of the National Library and Museum; Guillermo Tolentino, sculptor; Dr. Sixto de los Angeles, head of the medico-legal department of the University of the Philippines, and Eulogio B. Rodriguez, assistant director of the National Library. The group examined and verified the authenticity of the hero's remains.

The remains, along those of Marcelo H. del Pilar, were lost during the Battle of Manila in 1945. *Lost.*

But the authenticity of what is called "Bonifacio's bones" is once again contested because at the time of their discovery, Manuel Quezon was at loggerheads with Emilio Aguinaldo, who was going to run for president of the commonwealth. This is saying that a political taint places the remains under suspicion despite the autopsy and the verification of a diverse group.

The hero, destitute in life and death, is going to be deprived of his bones as well. The final step is to deny his spirit.

For a while, anyway, the hero, the tragic figure of the Revolution, had his day. Prodded by Masangkay, the outstanding Tagalog writer, Senator Lope K. Santos, sponsored a bill designating the 30th of November every year as *Bonifacio Day*. The preamble of Legislative Act No. 2946 of 9 February 1921 written in the beautiful Tagalog of "Lopeka," hailed Bonifacio as the *Hero of Deed* to Rizal's the *Hero of Thought*.

Fifteen years later, the loyal Masangkay started a civic movement that led to the construction of the national Bonifacio monument in Caloocan.

But in 1930, Act No. 3827 changed Bonifacio Day into National Heroes' Day. This was subsequently repealed and the old name reinstated, and yet now we still observe National Heroes' Day on 30 November. Some unknown, powerful force seems to be hounding the hero even beyond the grave.

The question is, borrowing from the Katipunan's words, *What is to be Done?* The dead had done their deed; they are no longer accountable. Yet we, the living, are haunted, and we can only extricate ourselves by indifference and forgetfulness, at the cost of making a mockery of our celebratory recollections of the last hundred years.

The Centenary was a celebration of a century of subterfuge, as we congratulated ourselves for the "good things" above a shameful episode in our history.

In a futile attempt to explain away the tragedy, so many scholars, writers, and historians are trying to convince us of the culpability of regionalism and elitism—at least in those times. But Masangkay was a Caviteño himself and did not see the fate of the hero as the result of a "struggle" between Caviteños and Manileños. As for the elites who despised Bonifacio, Julio Nakpil himself was one. Emilio Jacinto, though of the urban poor, was better educated than the conspirators of Tejeros.

The fact is that the persecutors turned prosecutors and executioners of the hero were individuals with their *personal* feelings about Andres Bonifacio. It would be an exaggeration to credit them with noble feelings in determining his fate, even if in the end some of them later fell as patriots fighting for their country. These personal feelings cannot just be explained away as regionalism, elitism, or some sort of superiority complex about the one man who made the Revolution that some held so dearly and others not-so-dearly.

But more than the inaccessible accountability of the hero's executioners is this generation's own responsibility towards the memory of the Hero, a memory that must be liberated from the continuing desecration.

Acknowledging the tragedy and confronting the shame are our only catharsis as presumed heirs of the Revolution. Regrettably, it will be nearly impossible to exact retribution, not with the way that History has turned out for us.

There is probably one thing that we can absolutely do: redeem the spirit and memory of Andres Bonifacio, and in so doing, liberate him from the Tragedy of the Philippine Revolution.

It was not a misunderstanding or mistake. It was not necessary for the life of the Revolution. It was not an inevitable unfolding of the historical process. It was a crime, even if historical time (whatever that means) decreed there were no criminals.

Some would counsel burying the tragedy in the past where it belongs, but history is about remembering, not forgetting. In writing this book, I obviously intended to keep the memory of the hero and our own tragedy alive, for there are lessons to be learned from this saga. But I did not intend that we reconstitute ourselves into factions, as did the Magdiwang and the Magdalo, but rather to recognize our unity as a people.

The retribution for the crime committed against our authentic hero probably had come without our knowing it. In any case, a hundred years should render it impossible.

The burden of history, I hold, remains with the living, and above all, on the descendants of the players, whatever their roles, in the historical drama. If they can learn to forgive one another, then we as a people can forgive ourselves.

Never again, we pray, shall we betray one another.

According to an Insider

Lt. Manuel Sityar (1863-1927) was born and raised in the Philippines by a Spanish father and Filipino mother. As head of the guardia civil stationed in Pasig, Sityar was among the first to discover the existence of the Katipunan. He reported to the governor-general that men were being enlisted by an unknown organization with initiates signing oaths in their own blood. Sityar gave an account of men actively recruiting from the neighboring towns of Mandaluyong and San Juan del Monte, and gathering arms in readiness for a revolution with the assistance of Japan.

Sityar was tasked to pursue these *filibusteros*. In a dramatic turn of events, the lieutenant had a change of heart and instead pledged loyalty to the revolutionary forces. He is said to have declared: "I have already served my father well; I will now serve my mother."

Sityar joined the forces of Emilio Aguinaldo and later served as his aide de camp. He was a member of the Malolos Congress which approved the first Philippine Constitution and eventually gave rise to Asia's first constitutional democracy. After the Revolution, Sityar taught at the Liceo de Manila and became a close personal friend of President Manuel L. Quezon.

Lt. Manuel Sityar's handwritten memoirs cover a ride range of topics and events relating to the Revolution. His diary contains first-hand accounts of an insider who occupied sensitive positions of power and authority,and witnessed and participated in the dramatic events of the Revolution. Following is a translation of the pertinent sections from his extant memoirs:

> *At the outset of the year 1897, as the Spanish troops were about to enter Silang to crush the revolution in Cavite, a consultation was held among the officials of the revolution under the leadership of Andres Bonifacio at the convent of San Francisco de Malabon where the* Supremo *was in residence. In this gathering, there arose a contentious discussion concerning the defense plans proposed by Bonifacio as opposed to that which other leaders from Cavite wanted. Due to a lack of consensus on what to do, Emilio Aguinaldo left the meeting disgruntled and was followed by other rebel soldiers.*
>
> *Toward midnight that evening, Andres Bonifacio, accompanied by about 200 followers some of whom were armed, left San Francisco de Malabon and headed in the direction of Silang, bringing with them the funds of the Revolution consisting of ten thousand Mexican pesos which they had kept at the convent that served as their Central Treasury.*
>
> *When Aguinaldo learned of the flight of Bonifacio, he ordered General Tomas Mascardo to pursue him and to capture him, dead or alive. Aguinaldo planned to surrender Bonifacio to the Spanish General Lachambre. Mascardo brought with him a force more or less equal to that under the command of* El Supremo.

Realizing that he was being pursued by Mascardo and knowing that he could not avoid an encounter as his destination was out of reach, Andres Bonifacio sought refuge in the barrio of Alulut, in the town of Indang. It was here where the two factions met in combat and where the Supremo *was resoundingly defeated, suffering a wound in the clavicle inflicted by a sword and being taken prisoner together with his young brother Procopio who was about 17 years old. Since Mascardo did not have the opportunity to kill Bonifacio in actual combat, he dispatched a soldier to deal him the lethal blow.*

Bonifacio was carried on a hammock toward the town of Naic where they formed a Council of War which would try him and sentence him to death by firing squad at the earliest possible time.

Setting the Record Straight

What is the measure of a man's greatness and when is he considered a national hero?

According to the National Historical Institute, there are three prerequisites before one can be recognized as a national hero, namely:

1. a law must be passed setting aside one day annually to be observed as a national holiday to honor the hero;
2. a national monument must be erected in memory of the hero by virtue of an enabling legislation; and
3. the hero must be nationally recognized as may be evidenced by the nationwide use of street names honoring the hero, as well as the erection of other minor monuments and markers in his memory.

On 9 February 1921, the Senate (of the Philippine Commonwealth Government) enacted Legislative Act No. 2946 proclaiming November 30 (the birth date of Andres Bonifacio) of each year as *Araw ni Bonifacio* (Bonifacio Day) and observing it as a national holiday all over the land, to honor the greatness and heroism of this "man of action" who founded the Katipunan and launched the revolutionary movement to free the country from foreign domination.

The above law followed a Legislative Act No. 2760 on 23 February 1918, approving the erection of a national monument in memory of Andres Bonifacio. Fifteen years later, the Bonifacio landmark done by famous sculptor Guillermo Tolentino was unveiled on 30 November 1933 in Balintawak.

Street names, other minor monuments, and markers all over the nation honor Andres Bonifacio and complete the three pre-requisites laid down; yet, the singular distinction recognizing him as a national hero has eluded this great man through a century of historical neglect.

Meanwhile, Legislative Act No. 3827 was passed on 28 October 1931 declaring the last Sunday of August as National Heroes' Day.

Although these two national holidays (last Sunday of August and November 30) were clearly intended by the legislators to be observed separately, there appears to be a persistent effort to consolidate these two commemorative holidays into one, sometimes to the exclusion and non-observance of Bonifacio Day on November 30.

This occurrence was first observed in three successive years during the Japanese occupation of the Philippines (1942-1944) as may be seen clearly from the editorials and newspaper accounts of *The Tribune* issues of November 30th of these years. Was this a matter of historical oversight or was it an attempt to erase the memory of a great man?

Even today, to the man on the street, November 30 is National Heroes' Day, notwithstanding clarificatory circulars reportedly issued by the National Historical Institute that it is not. Thanks to innumerable corporate calendars printed yearly for mass distribution, this error is regrettably perpetuated and has further added to the confusion.

On the occasion of Bonifacio's centennial, it is time to set the record straight and give honor where it is due. November 30 is ***Bonifacio Day***. And our great and beloved hero, Andres Bonifacio, should be affirmed and honored as a national hero of the Philippines.

The Naic Military Agreement

We who signed these presents with our true names, all officers of the Army who have met in convention headed by the Supreme Chief, on account of the critical situation of the *pueblos* and the war, having discovered the treason committed by certain officers who have been sowing discord and connived with the Spaniards, our enemies, corrupting the army and being guilty of criminal neglect in the care of the wounded, have agreed to deliver the people from this grave danger by means hereinafter enumerated,

First. All combatants shall, by persuasion or force, be incorporated in an army corps and placed under the command of General Pio del Pilar.

Second. We shall recognize no one as being vested with full power except Right in the first place, and then those courageous officers who, since the beginning of the war and until the present moment, have never gone back on their oath and have conducted themselves loyally.

Third, Any disloyal person shall be punished on the spot, according to his deserts.

Such is our agreement, and we swear before God and the country of our birth that we shall keep it unto the grave.

The Acta de Tejeros

Here at Tejeros, within the jurisdictional limits of the *pueblo* of *Mapagtiis*, of the capital *Magdiwang*, this 23rd day of March, 1897, I, the Minister of State and Acting President, Sr. Jacinto Lumbreras, Pueblo Nuebo, and the Members of the Cabinet Generals, Marshal, Brigadiers, Colonels, Presidents and other Chiefs of the *pueblos* within jurisdictional limits of the aforesaid capital, with the offices in which they are vested, competent and of legal age, in convention assembled, and Messrs. Andres Bonifacio, *Maypagasa*, Venerated Supremo; Mariano Alvarez, *Mainam*, the present President, do covenant:

First. That as regards the election of a President, Ministers, Generals, and other necessary officers, we have come to an agreement with those of the other Presidency of the capital *Magdalo;* in witness whereof we have held said election yesterday at Tejeros, but we cannot accept the result thereof because the same lacks legality, we have learned that actual pressure has been brought to bear upon our Presidency; and that the ballots have been prepared by one sole person and have been issued to unqualified persons in order to secure a majority; and we have learned that they have conspired there. For this reason we deny the validity of the action taken, the unlawfulness whereof is proved by the fact that they have been unable to prepare a formal minute-record for our signatures, aside from the capital defect that our brother officers were not present there and were outside.

Second. We have discovered their underhanded efforts for the purpose of putting our Presidents under their orders by boldly doing that which is prohibited: General Emilio Aguinaldo, invited our Presidents to consider things not mentioned in the printed letter, for reasons not known to us, because no notice of it has been received in our capital.

Third. That upon the capture by the Spaniards of Silang and Dasmariñas, *pueblos* of their jurisdiction, many of our soldiers were slain, and in addition to our having contributed money, animals and rice, we had many wounded and suffered other losses, thanks to God, no *pueblo* under our jurisdiction has fallen into the hands of the said enemy.

Fourth. That we have never solicited aid from them, while they have constantly been requesting it from us.

Fifth. That our men have been fighting the enemy practically all day and night in order to liberate them, aside from other most valuable services, as a reward for which they have attempted to snatch our Presidency away from us.

Sixth. That we were in fact the first to raise the standard of rebellion and the same after. And inasmuch as we are convinced that their actions are not those of true brethren, we have agreed to separate from them and that they shall not put our capital under their orders, happen what may, it being they, at all event, who should submit, seeing that they have caused all the trouble. We sign these presents, binding ourselves under oath to respond with our lives and property for the liberty and tranquility of our aforesaid Presidency; that we all and those who are with us and may desire to do so, will abide by the terms of this present covenant; that any misfortune that may happen to us, openly or secretly or any violent death, will be investigated by us and no effort will be spared until the guilty party is found, if there be any, and punished as he deserves; and we further covenant that if any person among us violated this compact, all will turn against him without pity; likewise, that we will make all efforts to trace the steps of those who may intend to commit treason against the Highest and Most Respectable Society, against the capital, or against our brethren, and that we will pursue them relentlessly and send them to the Presidency for punishment as soon as practicable. We conclude this compact in the name of the Most Venerable Society, all signing with our full names and our surnames in said Society; and though many, yet we are one in sentiment, in valor, in mutual cooperation, in disgrace, and in life. This document shall be safely guarded in the Presidency and printed copies of it shall be sent to the *pueblos* thereof who are of the same opinion, and shall be safely kept by the Presidents, brethren or their officers. Given on the day, month, and year above written.

Signed by Andres Bonifacio, Mariano Alvarez, Artemio Ricarte, Diego Moxica, and others, altogether 44 signatures.

Decalogue
Duties of the Sons of the People

1. Love God with all your heart.

2. Always remember that love of God demands love of the country of your birth, and this expresses itself in true love for fellowman.

3. Inscribe in your heart the hope for the sublime honor and destiny— that of dying for the sake of liberating your country.

4. Your aspirations will be crowned with success if accompanied by tranquility, determination, patience and faith.

5. Preserve the mandates and aims of the K.K.K. as you guard your honor.

6. All are mandated to give whatever is required to come to the aid of a brother who is at risk in the performance of his duty,

7. Be sensitive to others, and through your faithfulness and devotion to duty, set a good example to them.

8. Within your ability, share your resources with the poor and the downtrodden.

9.   Diligence in your work is borne out of your love for your own self, your wife and children, for your brothers and for your countrymen.

10.   Reward the good, and punish the evil. Believe, likewise, that the path of the K.K.K. is within the will of God and therefore, the will of the people is part of God's divine plan.

Bonifacio's Letters to Emilio Jacinto

Bro. Pedernal.

As regards the person from whom, according to you, the revolver will have to be taken, nobody knows him here; and the Captain Mariano whom you mention has perished in the engagement of Aromahan.

If you have to write me anything secretly, we must use the key of the second degree, because I usually receive your letters open here.

It has been possible to get only 800 ready cartridges, though we are allowed 1,000 and even 2,000 here in Magdiwang, in exchange for your aid there, because since the fighting here shows no sign of abating, we are running short of cartridges, and nothing has as yet been done than that.

As soon as you have signed the power, have the bearer take it immediately where it must go.

Your brother,

ANDRES BONIFACIO
Maypagasa

(March 8, 1897)

Sr. Emilio Jacinto Pedernal.

Mr. Chief of the Army—The disturbances here and the entrance of the enemy in the pueblos of Silang, P. Dasmariñas, Bacoor, Imus, Kawit, Noveleta, Malabon, Tanza, and Salinas* have not left me any leisure for writing you and replying to your letters; however I shall endeavor to do so and the bearer of the letter shall be our brother Sr. Antonino Guevara, who has most important things to communicate to you.

I received what you sent me: two cans of powder, a *bayong* of cartridge shells, and thirty pesos. The letter says 50, but only 30 were delivered to me, as I am informed that Brother Nakpil took the 20 pesos again.

The frequent attacks by the enemy on the pueblos above mentioned are due to the lack of unity and the customary dissension among leaders, who remain obstinate, although the people are having a terrible time to it.

Captain Emilio has received a letter sent by a Jesuit called Pio Pi and a Spaniard by the name of Rafael Comenge,** this was before the capture of Imus, and in the letter the revolutionary chiefs are invited to lay down their arms and are promised a general pardon. Captain Emilio made several conditions: expulsion of the friars, deputies to the Cortes, and others, and endorsed the matter to Mr. Alvarez, requesting his assent. Alvarez consulted me, and as we did not assent, those of Imus had Aguinaldo write secretly to the chiefs of the pueblos under Magdiwang.

When President Mariano learned of this, he called a meeting of the people and asked them what was the general desire, and at that meeting it was resolved to continue the war against the Spaniards and not to admit any terms of conciliation. At said meeting, it was further decided to establish a revolutionary government, but the thing resulted in a fiasco, because they all discovered the game of the Magdalo people and the convention accomplished nothing.

Owing to the turmoil and the defeats, the inhabitants here became terror-stricken, and Tirona, Cailles, and Jose del Rosario, who were Minister of War, Lieutenant General and Director of War, surrendered to the Spaniards and were followed by many officers and inhabitants of the pueblos of Tanza, all Magdalo men.

On account of these defections, of which the host of Captain Emilio had knowledge, nearly all the brethren asked me on their knees to take them away from there, to which request I gave no heed, as I was moved to compassion by the sad plight of so many citizens who, without being guilty, would suffer untold hardships and death.

The Batangas people have placed themselves under the orders of the Supreme Council, recognizing our authority; they will within three days begin to invade eight pueblos. For this undertaking they requested my assistance, and I gave them 20 riflemen and 20 bolomen, under the orders of Brother Artemio Ricarte.

A provincial government has already been established in Batangas; its general is called D. Miguel Malvar and he is a very intelligent man, better, perhaps than the general we know here, of Tanway.***

In case they should be successful in taking the pueblo of Lipa, one of the 8 pueblos to be invaded, they wish me to establish myself there, in order to be able, as they say, to carry the war into Camarines. For this reason, I wish to know from you whether I am more badly needed there, because I shall go there; otherwise I will remain in Batangas.

It is really necessary for us to agree upon the movement for the purpose of generalizing the war and carrying it everywhere. I therefore desire to know whether you have already gone to Bulacan and Nueva Ecija, and if not, I shall leave somebody in charge here and we shall go there; because if we do not bestir ourselves, you know that Mamerto Natividad is there, who will be doing what he did here; talk ill of us.

The arms have not yet arrived, and this delay is one of the causes which retain me here. Your mother is at Marigondon with a relative of hers there, and no mishap whatsoever has occurred to her.

Receive my affectionate embrace,

The C. Sup.,
ANDRES BONIFACIO
Maypagasa

(April 16, 1897)

*Revolutionary name of the town of Rosario
**President of the Casino Español
***Obviously referring to General Emilio Aguinaldo

Bibliography and Readings

Agoncillo, Teodoro A. *Revolt of the Masses: The Story of Bonifacio and the Katipunan* (U. P. Quezon City: 1956).

—————. *The Writings and Trial of Andres Bonifacio*. Collected and translated with the collaboration of S. V. Epistola of the Ravens.

Alvarez, Santiago V. *Ang Katipunan at ang Himagsikan*. English translation by Paula Carolina S. Malay as *The Katipunan and the Revolution: Memoirs of a General* (Ateneo de Manila Press: 1992).

Blair, Emma and James Robertson (eds.). *The Philippine Islands 1493-1898*. Vol. XIX (Cleveland, A. H. Clark Co., 1903-1909).

Bonifacio, Andres. "Ang Dapat Mabatid ng mga Tagalog," undated. From Jose P. Santos: *Si Andres Bonifacio at ang Himagsikan* (Manila: 1935), p. 67.

—————. "Katipunan Mararahas ng mga Anak ng Bayan," undated (released in the first quarter of 1897)at San Francisco Malabon or Mapagtiis. Printed leaflet in Pedro S. Achutegui, S. J. and Miguel A. Bernard, S. J. *Aguinaldo and the Revolution of 1896, A Documentary History* (Quezon City, Ateneo de Manila: 1972), pp. 328-32, and 570. The original was reported kept in the Dominican Archives.

—————. "Manifesto proclaiming Bulacan, Hagdang Bato in Mandaluyong, dated 28 August 1896." From Hermenegildo Cruz, *Kartilyang Makabayan* (Maynila, S. P.: 1912), p. 43.

Calairo, Emmanuel Franco. *Ladislao Diwa at ang Katipunan*.

Corpuz, O. D. *The Roots of the Filipino Nation*. Vol II (Quezon City, AKLAHI Foundation, Inc.: 1989).

De Jesus, Gregoria. "Mga Tala ng Aking Buhay." In *Julio Nakpil and the Philippine Revolution*. Edited and translated by Encarnacion Alzona (Manila, by the heirs of Julio Nakpil: 1954).

De los Santos, Epifanio. *The Revolutionists: Aguinaldo, Bonifacio, Jacinto*. Edited by Teodoro A. Agoncillo from a compilation translated by Eulogio M. Leano and Gregoria Nieva (Manila, National Historical Commission: 1973).

Guerrero, Milagros C. "Aguinaldo's Secret." *Filipinas*. November 1996.

————. "Andres Bonifacio and the 1896 Revolution" and "Balintawak: The Cry for a Nationwide Revolution," with Emmanuel N. Encarnacion and Ramon N. Villegas. *Sulyap Kultura*, second quarter (Quezon City: 1996).

Kalaw, Teodoro M. *The Philippine Revolution* (Mandaluyong, Rival. J. B. Vargas Filipino Foundation: 1969).

Mabini, Apolinario. *The Philippine Revolution*. Translated by Leon Ma. Guerrero (Manila: National Historical Commission:1969). *Letters*. Compiled and translated by the National Heroes Commission (Manila: 1965).

Makapagal's account in 1997 in Jose P. Santos, *Mga Kasulatang Lumiliwanag sa Pagkakapatay kay Andres Bonifacio* (Manila: 1935), pp. 40-41.

Minutes of the Katipunan (National Historical Institute: 1978).

Ricarte, Artemio. *Memoirs of General Artemio Ricarte*. Selected and edited from manuscripts in the Watson Collection (Manila, National Heroes Commission: 1963).

The Author

Considered by colleagues as *l'homme engagé*, Adrian E. Cristobal was a UP regent, vice-chairman of the "think tank," the Philippine Center for Advanced Studies, later known as the President's Center for Special Studies (of which he was executive director), professor in the UP Asian Center, presidential spokesman, and has served in various other official capacities. His other books are *Occasional Prose*, *Filipino First* (an approach to economic policy), *The Trial*, and *Pasquinades*. He is a SEAWRITE awardee, a Palanca prizewinner for drama and essay, and a recipient of "outstanding" awards in literature and political writing. He has been a columnist for the *Philippine Daily Inquirer*, publisher of the *Manila Times*, and is currently associate editor/columnist of the *Manila Bulletin* and executive publisher of the *Philippine Graphic* magazine.